GALLIPOLI

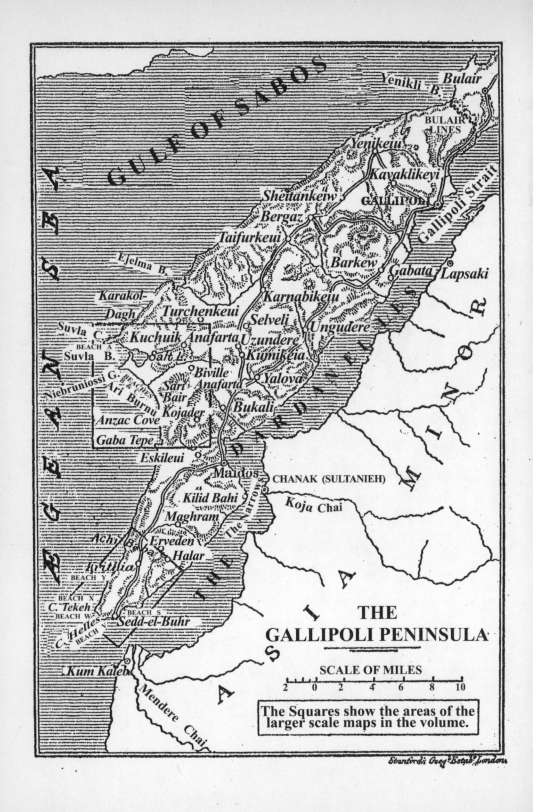

THE
GALLIPOLI PENINSULA

SCALE OF MILES

The Squares show the areas of the
larger scale maps in the volume.

GALLIPOLI

John Masefield

LARGE PRINT

Oxford

First published in Great Britain 1916
by Heinemann

Published in Large Print 2002 by ISIS Publishing Ltd.,
7 Centremead, Osney Mead, Oxford OX2 0ES
by arrangement with The Society of Authors

British Library Cataloguing in Publication Data
Masefield, John 1878–1967
Gallipoli. – Large print ed.
1. World War, 1914–1918 – Campaigns – Turkey –
Gallipoli Peninsula – Fiction
2. War stories 3. Large type books
I. Title
823.9'12 (F)

ISBN 0–7531–5625–3 (hb)
ISBN 0–7531–5626–1 (pb)

Printed and bound by Antony Rowe, Chippenham

DEDICATED WITH THE

DEEPEST ADMIRATION AND RESPECT

TO

GENERAL SIR IAN HAMILTON
G.C.B., D.S.O.,

AND THE

OFFICERS AND MEN UNDER HIS COMMAND

MARCH TO OCTOBER, 1915

CHAPTER
ONE

Oliver said: "I have seen the Saracens: the valley and the mountains are covered with them; and the lowlands and all the plains; great are the hosts of that strange people; we have here a very little company."
Roland answered: "My heart is the bigger for that. Please God and His holiest angels, France shall never lose her name through me."

— *The Song of Roland*.

A Little while ago, during a short visit to America, I was often questioned about the Dardanelles Campaign. People asked me why that attempt had been made, why it had been made in that particular manner, why other courses had not been taken, why this had been done and that either neglected or forgotten, and whether a little more persistence, here or there, would not have given us the victory.

These questions were often followed by criticism of various kinds, some of it plainly suggested by our enemies, some of it shrewd, and some the honest opinion of men and women happily ignorant of modern war. I answered questions and criticism as best I could, but in the next town they were repeated to me, and in the town beyond reiterated, until I wished that I had a printed leaflet, giving my views of the matter, to distribute among my questioners.

Later, when there was leisure, I began to consider the Dardanelles Campaign, not as a tragedy, nor as a mistake, but as a great human effort, which came, more than once, very near to triumph, achieved the impossible many times, and failed, in the end, as many great deeds of arms have failed, from something which had nothing to do with arms nor with the men who bore them. That the effort failed is not against it; much that is most splendid in military history failed, many great things and noble men have failed. To myself, this failure is the second grand event of the war; the first was Belgium's answer to the German ultimatum.

The Peninsula of Gallipoli, or Thracian Chersonese, from its beginning in the Gulf of Xeros to its extremity at Cape Helles, is a tongue of hilly land, about fifty-three miles long, between the Ægean Sea and the Straits of the Dardanelles. At its north-eastern, Gulf of Xeros, or European end, it is four or five miles broad; then, a little to the south of the town of Bulair, it narrows to three miles, in a contraction or neck which was fortified during the Crimean War by French and English soldiers. This fortification is known as the Lines of Bulair. Beyond these lines, to the south-west, the Peninsula broadens in a westward direction and attains its maximum breadth, of about twelve miles, some twenty-four miles from Bulair, between the two points of Cape Suvla, on the sea, and Cape Uzun, within the Straits. Beyond this broad part is a second contraction or neck, less than five miles across, and beyond this, pointing roughly west-south-westerly, is the final tongue or finger of the Peninsula, an isosceles triangle of land with a base of some seven miles, and two sides of thirteen miles each, converging in the blunt tip (perhaps a mile and a half across) between Cape Helles and Cape Tekke. There is no railway within the Peninsula, but bad roads, possible for wheeled traffic, wind in the valleys, skirting the hills and linking up the principal villages. Most of the travelling and commerce of the Peninsula is done by boat, along the Straits, between the little port of Maidos, near the Narrows, and the town of Gallipoli (the chief town) near the Sea of Marmora. From Gallipoli there is a fair road to Bulair and beyond. Some twenty other small towns or hamlets are scattered here and there in the well-watered valleys in the central broad portion of the Peninsula. The inhabitants are mostly small cultivators with olive and currant orchards, a few vineyards and patches of beans and grains; but not a hundredth part of the land is under cultivation.

The seashore, like the Straits shore, is mainly steep-to, with abrupt sandy cliffs rising from the sea to a height of from one hundred to three hundred feet. At irregular and rare intervals these cliffs are broken by the ravines or gullies down which the autumnal and winter rains escape; at the sea mouths of these gullies are sometimes narrow strips of stony or sandy beach.

Viewed from the sea, the Peninsula is singularly beautiful. It rises and falls in gentle and stately hills between four hundred and eleven hundred feet high, the highest being at about the centre. In its colour (after the brief spring), in its gentle beauty, and the grace and austerity of its line, it resembles those parts of Cornwall to the north of Padstow from which one can see Brown Willie. Some Irish hills recall it. I know no American landscape like it.

In the brief spring the open ground is covered with flowers, but there is not much open ground. In the Cape Helles district it is mainly poor land growing heather and thyme; farther north there is abundant scrub, low shrubs and brushwood, from two to four feet high, frequently very thick. The trees are mostly stunted firs, not very numerous in the south, where the fighting was, but more frequent north of Suvla. In one or two of the villages there are fruit trees; on some of the hills there are small clumps of pine. Viewed from the sea the Peninsula looks waterless and sun-smitten; the few watercourses are deep ravines showing no water. Outwardly, from a distance, it is a stately land of beautiful graceful hills rolling in suave yet austere lines and covered with a fleece of brushwood. In reality the suave and graceful hills are exceedingly

4

steep, much broken and roughly indented with gullies, clefts, and narrow irregular valleys. The soil is something between a sand and a marl, loose and apt to blow about in dry weather when not bound down by the roots of brushwood, but sticky when wet.

Those who look at the south-western end of the Peninsula, between Cape Suvla and Cape Helles, will see three heights greater than the rolling wold or downland around them. Seven miles south-east from Cape Suvla is the great and beautiful peaked hill of Sari Bair, 970 feet high, very steep on its sea side and thickly fleeced with scrub. This hill commands the landing-place at Suvla. Seven miles south from Sari Bair is the long dominating plateau of Kilid Bahr, which runs inland from the Straits, at heights varying between five and seven hundred feet, to within two miles of the sea. This plateau commands the Narrows of the Hellespont. Five miles farther to the south-west and less than six miles from Cape Helles is the bare and lonely lump of Achi Baba, 590 feet high. This hill commands the landing-place at Cape Helles. These hills and the ground commanded by them were the scenes of some of the noblest heroism which ever went far to atone for the infamy of war. Here the efforts of our men were made.

Those who wish to imagine the scene must think of twenty miles of any rough and steep sea coast known to them, picturing it as roadless, waterless, much broken with gullies, covered with scrub, sandy, loose, and difficult to walk on, and without more than two miles of accessible landing throughout its length. Let them picture this familiar twenty miles as dominated at intervals by three hills bigger than the hills about them, the north hill a peak, the centre a ridge or plateau, and the south hill a lump. Then let them imagine the hills entrenched, the landing mined, the beaches tangled with barbed wire, ranged by howitzers and swept by machine guns, and themselves three thousand miles from home, going out before dawn, with rifles, packs, and water-bottles, to pass the mines under shell fire, cut through the wire under machine-gun fire, clamber up the hills under the fire of all arms, by the glare of shell-bursts, in the withering and crashing tumult of modern war, and then to dig themselves in a waterless and burning hill while a more numerous enemy charge them with the bayonet. And let them imagine themselves enduring this night after night, day after day, without rest or solace, nor respite from the peril of death, seeing their friends killed, and their position imperilled, getting their food, their munitions, even their drink, from the jaws of death, and their breath from the taint of death, and their brief sleep upon the dust of death. Let them imagine themselves driven mad by heat and toil and thirst by day, shaken by frost at midnight, weakened by disease and broken by pestilence, yet rising on the word with a shout and going forward to die in exultation in a cause foredoomed and almost hopeless. Only then will they begin, even dimly, to understand what our seizing and holding of the landings meant.

All down the south-eastern coast of this Peninsula or outlier from Europe is a channel of sea, known, anciently, as the Hellespont, but in modern times more generally as the Dardanelles, from old fortifications of that name near the south-western end of the Strait. This channel, two or three miles across at its south-western end, broadens rapidly to four or five, then narrows to two, then, for a short reach, to one mile or less, after which (with one more contraction) it maintains a steady breadth of two or three miles till it opens into the great salt lake of the Sea of Marmora, and thence by another narrow reach into the Black Sea, or Euxine.

It is a deep-water channel, with from twenty-five to fifty fathoms of water in it throughout its length. The Gallipoli, or European, shore is steep-to, with a couple of fathoms of water close inshore, save in one or two beaches where it shoals. On the Asian shore, where the ground is lower and the coast more shelving, the water is shallower. A swift current of from two to three knots an hour runs always down the channel from the Sea of Marmora; and this with a south-westerly gale against it makes a nasty sea.

This water of the Hellespont is the most important channel of water in the world. It is the one entrance and exit to the Black Sea, the mouths of the Danube, Dniester, Dnieper, and Don, and the great ports of Constantinople, Odessa, and

Sebastopol. He who controls the channel controls those ports, with their wealth and their power to affect great conflicts. The most famous war of all time was fought, not for any human Helen, but to control that channel. Our Dardanelles Campaign was undertaken to win through it a free passage for the ships of the Allied Powers.

While the war was still young it became necessary to attempt this passage for five reasons: (1) To break the link by which Turkey keeps her hold as a European Power. (2) To divert a large part of the Turkish army from operations against our Russian Allies in the Caucasus and elsewhere. (3) To pass into Russia, at a time when her northern ports were closed by ice, the rifles and munitions of war of which her armies were in need. (4) To bring out of Southern Russia the great stores of wheat lying there waiting shipment. (5) If possible, to prevent, by a successful deed of arms in the Near East, any new alliance against us among the Balkan peoples.

In its simplest form the problem was to force a passage through the defended channel of the Dardanelles into the Sea of Marmora, to attack the capital of Turkey in Europe, to win through the Bosphorus into the Black Sea, securing each step in the advance against reconquest by the Turks, so that ships might pass from the Ægean to the Russian ports in the Black Sea, bringing to the Russians arms for their unequipped troops and taking from them the corn of the harvests of Southern Russia.

The main problem was to force a passage through the defended channel of the Hellespont.

This passage had been forced in the past by a British naval squadron. In February, 1807, Sir John Duckworth sailed through with seven ships of the line and some smaller vessels, silenced the forts at Sestos and Abydos and destroyed some Turkish ships, and then, fearing that the Turks, helped by French engineers, would so improve the fortifications that he would never be able to get back, he returned. On his return, one of his ships, the *Endymion* frigate, 40 guns, received in her hull two stone shot each twenty-six inches in diameter.

The permanent fortifications guarding the channel were added to and improved during the nineteenth century. At the outbreak of the war with Italy, four years ago, they were equipped (perhaps by German officers) with modern weapons. An attempt made by Italian torpedo-boats to rush the Straits by night was discovered by searchlights and checked by a heavy fire from quick-firing and other guns. All the torpedo-boats engaged in the operations were hit and compelled to return.

When Turkey entered the war against the Allied Powers, her officers had every reason to expect that the British or French fleets would attempt to force the channel. The military prize, Constantinople and the control of the Black Sea (whether for peace or for offence), was too great a temptation to be resisted. Helped by their German allies, they prepared for this attack with skill, knowledge, and determination. The Turks had no effective battle fleet, as in the sixteenth century, when they sought their enemies upon their own coasts, and had they had one they could not have passed the British fleet blockading the Dardanelles; but they prepared the channel and its shores so that no enemy ship might pass to seek them.

More than the two great wars, in South Africa and Manchuria, the present war has shown:

(a) That in modern war defence is easier and less costly in men and munitions, however much less decisive, than attack;

(b) That the ancient type of permanent fortress, built of steel, concrete, and heavy masonry, is much less easy to defend against the fire of heavy modern howitzers and high explosives than temporary field works, dug into the earth and protected by earth and sand-bags;

(c) That the fire of modern long-range guns is wasteful and ineffective unless the object fired at can be accurately ranged, and the fire controlled by officers who can watch the bursting of the shells on or near the target;

(d) That in restricted waters the fixed or floating mine, filled with high explosive, is a sure defence against enemy ships.

Beginning with proposition (a), the Turks argued that (unlike most defences) a defence of the passage of the Dardanelles against naval attack might well be decisive (*i.e.*, that it might well cause the attack to be abandoned or even destroy the attacking ships), since ships engaged in the attack would be under every disadvantage.

(*b*) Their guns, however heavy, would not be over-whelmingly successful against temporary field works and gun emplacements.

(*c*) Their officers, unable in the first place to locate the guns hidden on the shore, would be unable to observe the effect of their fire, and therefore unable to direct it, and this disadvantage would become greater as the ships advanced within the channel and became shut in by the banks.

(*d*) They would be unable to enter the channel until the waters had been dragged for mines by mine-sweepers. The batteries of field guns hidden on the coast would perhaps be sufficient to stop the progress of the mine-sweepers. If not, floating mines, along-shore torpedo-tubes, and the accurately ranged and directed fire of heavy howitzers, would perhaps sink the ships of war as they advanced.

(*e*) A ship, if damaged, would be five hundred miles from any friendly dock and seven hundred miles from any friendly arsenal. Replenishments of ammunition, fuel, food and water would have to be brought to the attacking fleet across these distances of sea, past many islands, and through one or two channels well suited to be the lurking grounds for enemy submarines.

On the other hand, there was the possibility that the heavy naval guns would make the field works untenable; that observers in aeroplanes and seaplanes would locate, range, and observe the fire upon the hidden batteries; that thus the mine-sweepers would be able to clear a passage up the Straits without undue interruption, and complete the task demanded of them without military assistance.

Before operations could be begun by the Allied Fleets it was necessary to secure some harbour, as close as possible to the Straits, to serve as what is called an advanced or subsidiary base, where large stores of necessaries, such as fuel and munitions, could be accumulated for future use by the ships engaged.

The port of Mudros, in Lemnos, was selected as this subsidiary base. This great natural harbour, measuring some two by three miles across, provides good holding ground in from five to seven fathoms of water for half the ships in the world. Two islands in the fairway divide the entrance into three passages, and make it more easy for the naval officer to defend the approaches. It is a safe harbour for ocean-going ships in all weathers; but with northerly or southerly gales, such as spring up very rapidly there in the changeable seasons of the year, and blow with great violence for some hours at a time, the port is much wind-swept, and the sea makes it dangerous for boats to lie along-side ships. Mudros itself, the town from which the port is named, is a small collection of wretched houses inhabited by Levantines, who live by fishery, petty commerce, and a few olive gardens and vineyards. It has a cathedral or largish church, and a small wooden pier, without appliances, for the use of the native boatmen. The town lies to the east of the harbour, on some rising ground or sand which stands up a little higher than the surrounding country. Behind it, rather more than a mile away, are barren hills of some eight hundred or nine hundred feet. The port is ringed in with these hills; it looks like a great extinct crater flooded by the sea. Over the hills in fair weather the peaks of Samothrace can be seen. When the spring flowers have withered the island is of the colour of a lion's skin. Its only beauty then is that of changing light.

Mudros in itself offered nothing to the Allied Fleets but a safe anchorage. It could not even supply the ships with fresh water, let alone meat, bread, and vegetables. The island produces little for its few inhabitants; its wealth of a few goats, fish, olives, and currants could be bought up in a week by the crew of one battleship. Everything necessary for the operations had therefore to be brought by sea and stored in Mudros till wanted. When this is grasped, the difficulties of the undertaking will be understood. There was no dock, wharf, nor crane in Mudros, nor any place in the harbour where a dock or wharf could be built without an immense labour of dredging. Ships could not be repaired nor dry-docked there, nor could they discharge and receive heavy stores save by their own winches and derricks. Throughout the operations ships had to serve as wharves, and ships' derricks as cranes, and goods were shipped, reshipped, and transhipped by that incessant manual labour which is the larger half of war.

Early in 1915, it was decided that a naval force should attempt the passage of the Straits.

On the 18th of February and following days, the Allied Fleets attacked the forts at the entrance to the Straits and soon silenced them. These were old-fashioned stone structures of great strength; they were knocked about and made untenable by the fire from the ships, but not destroyed. After this first easy success came delay, for the real obstacles lay within the Straits, between Cape Helles and the Narrows. Here, at intervals, very skilfully laid, commanded by many guns, ranged to the inch, were eight big mine-fields, stretching almost across the navigable channel in different directions. No ships could pass this part of the Straits until the mines had been groped for and removed. In thick and violent weather, under heavy fire, and troubled by the strong current, the mine-sweepers began to remove them, helped by the guns of the fleet. But the fleet's fire could not destroy the mobile field guns and howitzers hidden in the gullies and nullahs (invisible from the ships) on the Asian shore and to the east of Achi Baba. The Boers, and, later, the Japanese, had shown how difficult it is to locate well-concealed guns. Even when sea and aeroplanes had seen and signalled the whereabouts of the hidden guns, the ships could only fire at the flashes and at most hit some of the gunners; if their fire became too accurate, the gunners would retire to their shelters, or withdraw their guns to new hidden emplacements. These hidden guns, firing continually upon the mine-sweepers, made the clearing of the mine-fields towards the Narrows a slow and bloody task.

On the 18th of March, the ships developed a fierce fire upon the shore defences, and in the midst of the engagement the Turks floated some large mines upon the attacking ships, and by these means sank three battleships, one French, two English, the French ship with all her crew.

Heavy and unsettled weather, which made mine-sweeping impossible, broke off serious operations for some days. During these days it was decided, though with grave misgivings among the counsellors, that an army should be landed on the Peninsula to second the next naval attack.

It was now a month since the operations had begun, and the original decision, to leave the issue solely to the ships, had delayed the concentration of the troops needed for the task. The army, under the supreme command of General Sir Ian Hamilton, was assembling, but not yet concentrated nor on the scene. Some of it was in Egypt, some in transports at sea. When it was decided to use the army in the venture, much necessary work had still to be done. The Turks had now been given so much time to defend the landing-places that to get our troops ashore at all called for the most elaborate

15

preparation and the working out of careful schemes with the naval officers. The Germans boasted that our troops would never be able to land; possibly at first thought many soldiers would have agreed with them. But English soldiers and sailors are not Germans; they are, as Carlyle says, "far other"; our Admirals and General felt that with courage and a brave face our troops could land. It was true that the well-armed Turks were amply ready, and could easily concentrate against any army which we could land and supply a far larger force, more easily supplied and supported. But in the narrow Peninsula they could not move their larger forces so as to outflank us. Our flanks could be protected always by the fleet. And besides in war, fortune plays a large part, and skill, courage, and resolution, and that fine blending of all three in the uncommon sense called genius, have often triumphed even where common sense has failed. It was necessary that we should divert large armies of Turks from our Russian allies in the Caucasus; it was desirable to strike the imaginations of the Balkan States by some daring feat of arms close to them; it was vital to our enterprise in Mesopotamia and to the safety of Egypt that we should alarm the Turks for their capital and make them withdraw their armies from their frontiers. This operation, striking at the heart of the Turkish Empire, was the readiest way to do all these things.

The army designed for this honourable and dangerous task consisted of the following:

A division of French soldiers, the Corps Expéditionnaire de l'Orient, under M. le General d'Amade. This division was made up of French Territorial soldiers and Senegalese.

The 29th Division of British regular troops.

The Royal Naval Division.

The Australian and New Zealand Army Corps.

The French Division and the 29th Division of British Regular soldiers were men who had been fully trained in time of peace, but the Australian and New Zealand Army Corps and the Royal Naval Division, who together made up more than half the army, were almost all men who had enlisted since the declaration of war, and had had not more than six months' active training. They were, however, the finest body of young men ever brought together in modern times. For physical beauty and nobility of bearing they surpassed any men I have ever seen; they walked and looked like the kings in old poems, and reminded me of the line in Shakespeare:

"Baited like eagles having lately bathed."

As their officers put it, "they were in the pink of condition and didn't care a damn for anybody." Most of these new and irregular formations were going into action for the first time, to receive their baptism of fire in "a feat of arms only possible to the flower of a very fine army."

Having decided to use the army, the question how to use it was left to the commanding General, whose task was to help the British fleet through the Narrows. Those who have criticized the operations to me, even those who knew or pretended to know the country and military matters (but who were, for the most part, the gulls or agents of German propaganda), raised, nearly always, one or both of the following alternatives to the attack used by Sir Ian Hamilton. They have asked:

1. Why did he not attack at or to the north of Bulair in the Gulf of Xeros? or
2. Why did he not attack along the Asiatic coast instead of where he did, at Cape Helles and Anzac?

Those who have asked these questions have always insisted to me that had he chosen either alternative his efforts must have been successful. It may be well to set down here the final and sufficient reasons against either folly.

Firstly, then, the reasons against landing the army at or to the north of Bulair in the Gulf of Xeros.

The task demanded of the army was to second the naval attack in the Straits — *i.e.*, by seizing and occupying, if possible, that high ground in the Peninsula from which the Turkish guns molested the mine-sweepers. As this high ground commanded the Asiatic shore, its occupation by the British troops would have made possible the passage of the Straits. This and this alone was the task demanded of the army; no adventure upon Constantinople was designed or possible with the numbers of men available. How the army could have seconded the naval attack by landing three or four days' march from the Narrows within easy reach of the large Turkish armies in European Turkey is not clear.

Nevertheless, our task was to land the army, and all landing-places had to be examined. Pass now to —

(*a*) Bulair was carefully reconnoitred, and found to be a natural stronghold, so fortified with earthworks that there was no chance of taking it. Ten thousand Turks had been digging there for a month, and had made it impregnable. There are only two landing-places near Bulair: one (a very bad one) in a swamp or salt marsh to the east, the other in a kind of death-trap ravine to the west, both dominated by high ground in front, and one (the eastward) commanded also from the rear. Had the army, or any large part of it, landed at either beach, it would have been decimated in the act and then held up by the fortress.

(*b*) Had the army landed to the north of Bulair on the coast of European Turkey, it would have been in grave danger of destruction. Large Turkish armies could have marched upon its left and front from Adrianople and Rodosto, while, as it advanced, the large army in Gallipoli, reinforced from Asia across the Straits, could have marched from Bulair and fallen upon its right flank and rear.

(c) But even had it beaten these armies, some four times its own strength, it would none the less have perished, through failure of supplies, since no European army could hope to live upon a Turkish province in the spring, and European supplies could have been brought to it only with the utmost difficulty and danger. There is no port upon that part of the Turkish coast; no shelter from the violent southerly gales, and no depth of water near the shore. In consequence, no transports of any size could approach within some miles of the coast to land either troops or stores. Even had there been depth of water for them, transports could not have discharged upon the coast because of the danger from submarines. They would have been compelled to discharge in the safe harbour of the subsidiary base at Mudros in Lemnos, and (as happened with the fighting where it was) their freight, whether men or stores, reshipped into small ships of too light draught to be in danger from submarines, and by them conveyed to the landing-places. But this system, which never quite failed at Anzac and Cape Helles, would have failed on the Xeros coast. Anzac is some forty miles from Mudros, the Xeros coast is eighty, or twice the distance. Had the army landed at Xeros, it would have been upon an un-productive enemy territory in an unsettled season of the year, from eight to twenty hours' steam from their one safe subsidiary base. A stormy week might have cut them off at any time from all possibility of obtaining a man, a biscuit, a cartridge, or even a drink of water, and this upon ground where they could with little trouble be outnumbered by armies four times their strength with sound communications.

Secondly, for the reasons against attacking along the Asiatic coast —

(*a*) The coast is commanded from the Gallipoli coast, and therefore less important to those trying to second a naval attack upon the Narrows.

(*b*) An army advancing from Kum Kale along the Asiatic shore would be forced to draw its supplies from oversea. As it advanced, its communications could be cut with great ease at any point by the hordes of armed Turks in Asia Minor.

(*c*) The Turkish armies in Asia Minor would have attacked it in the right and rear, those from Bulair and Rodosto would have ferried over and attacked it in front, the guns in Gallipoli would have shelled its left, and the task made impracticable.

Some of those who raised these alternatives raised a third when the first two had been disposed of. They asked, "Even if the army could not have landed at Bulair or on the Asian coast, why did it land where it did land, on those suicidal beaches?" The answer to this criticism is as follows: It landed on those beaches because there were no others on the Peninsula, because the only landing-places at which troops could be got ashore with any prospect of success, however slight, were just those three or four small beaches near Cape Helles, at the south-west end of the Peninsula, and the one rather longer beach to the north of Gaba or Kaba Tepe. All these beaches were seen to be strongly defended, with barbed-wire entanglements on the shore and under the water, with sea and land mines, with strongly entrenched riflemen, many machine guns, and an ample artillery. In addition, the beaches close to Cape Helles were within range of big guns mounted near Troy on the Asian shore, and the beach near Gaba Tepe was ranged by the guns in the olive-groves to the south and on the hills to the north of it. A strong Turkish army held the Peninsula, and very powerful reserves were at Bulair, all well supplied (chiefly by boat from the Asian shore) with food and munitions. German officers had organized the defence of the Peninsula with great professional skill. They had made it a fortress of great strength, differing from all other fortresses in this, that besides being almost impregnable it was almost unapproachable. But our army had its task to do, there was no other means of doing it, and our men had to do what they could. Anyone trying to land, to besiege that fortress, had to do so by boat or lighter under every gun in the Turkish army. The Turks and the Germans knew, better than we, what few and narrow landing-places were possible to our men; they had had more than two months of time in which to make those landing-places fatal to any enemy within a mile of them, yet our men came from three thousand miles away, passed that mile of massacre, landed and held on with all their guns, stores, animals, and appliances, in spite of the Turk and his ally, who outnumbered them at every point.

No army in history has made a more heroic attack; no army in history has been set such a task. No other body of men in any modern war has been called upon to land over mined and wired waters under the cross fire of machine guns. The Japanese at Chinampo and Chemulpho were not opposed, the Russians at Pitzewo were not prepared, the Spaniards at Daiquiri made no fight. Our men achieved a feat without parallel in war, and no other troops in the world (not even Japanese or Ghazis in the hope of heaven) would have made good those beaches on the 25th of April.

CHAPTER
TWO

Then said Roland: "Oliver, companion, brother
. . . we shall have a strong and tough battle,
such as man never saw fought. But I shall
strike with my sword, and you, comrade, will
strike with yours; we have borne our swords in
so many lands, we have ended so many
battles with them, that no evil song shall be
sung of them . . ." At these words the Franks
went forward gladly.

— *The Song of Roland*.

Let the reader now try to imagine the nature of the
landing. In order to puzzle the Turkish commander,
to make him hesitate and divide his forces, it was
necessary to land or pretend to land, in some force,
simultaneously at various places. A feint of landing
was to be made near Bulair; the French Corps
Expéditionnaire was to land at Kum Kale, to attack
and silence the Asiatic fortifications and batteries;
the Australian and New Zealand Army Corps was
to land at or near Gaba Tepe; while men of the 29th
and Royal Naval Divisions landed at or near Cape
Helles, some towards Krithia on the north, others

nearer Sedd-el-Bahr on the south-west and south. The main attacks were to be those near Gaba Tepe and Cape Helles.

At Cape Helles three principal landings were to be made at the following places:

1. At Beach V, a small semicircular sandy bay, three hundred yards across, just west of the ruins of Sedd-el-Bahr castle. The ground rises steeply round the half-circle of the bay exactly as the seats rise in an amphitheatre. Modern defence could not ask for a more perfect site.

2. At Beach W (to the west of V), where a small sandy bay, under Cape Tekke, offered a landing upon a strip of sand about the size of Beach V. The slope upward from this beach is more gentle than at V, through a succession of sand-dunes, above which the ground was strongly entrenched. The cliffs north and south are precipitous, and make the beach a kind of gully or ravine. The Turks had placed machine guns in holes in the cliff, had wired and mined both beach and bay, and thrown up strong redoubts to flank them. Beach W was a death trap.

3. At Beach X (north of W, on the other or northern side of Cape Tekke), a narrow strip of sand, two hundred yards long, at the foot of a low cliff. This, though too small to serve for the quick passage ashore of many men at a time, was a slightly easier landing-place than the other two, owing to the lie of the ground.

Besides these main landings, two minor landings were to be made as follows:

4. At Beach S, a small beach, within the Straits, beyond Sedd-el-Bahr.

5. At Beach Y (on the Ægean, to the west of Krithia), a strip of sand below a precipitous cliff, gashed with steep, crumbling, and scrub-covered gullies.

These two minor landings were to protect the flanks of the main landing parties, "to disseminate the forces of the enemy and to interrupt the arrival of his reinforcements." They were to take place at dawn (at about 5a.m. or half an hour before the main attacks), without any preliminary bombardment from the fleet upon the landing-places.

Near Gaba Tepe only one landing was to be made, upon a small beach, two hundred yards across, a mile to the north of Gaba Tepe promontory. The ground beyond this beach is abrupt sandy cliff, covered with scrub, flanked by Gaba Tepe, and commanded by the land to shoreward.

For some days before the landing the army lay at Mudros, in Lemnos, aboard its transports, or engaged in tactical exercises ashore and in the harbour. Much bitter and ignorant criticism has been passed upon this delay, which was, unfortunately, very necessary. The month of April, 1915, in the Ægean, was a month of unusually unsettled weather; it was quite impossible to attempt the landing without calm water and the likelihood of fine weather for some days. In rough weather it would have been impossible to land laden soldiers with their stores through the surf of open beaches under heavy fire, and those who maintain that "other soldiers" (*i.e.*, themselves) would have made the attempt can have no knowledge of what wading ashore from a boat, in bad weather, in the Ægean or any other sea, even without a pack and with no enemy ahead, is like. But in unsettled weather the Gallipoli coast is not only difficult, but exceedingly dangerous for small vessels. The currents are fierce, and a short and ugly sea gets up quickly and makes towing hazardous. Had the attempt been made in foul weather a great many men would have been drowned, some few would have reached the shore, and then the ships would have been forced off the coast. The few men left on the shore would have had to fight there with neither supplies nor supports till the enemy overwhelmed them.

Another reason for delay was the need for the most minute preparation. Many armies have been landed from boats from the time of Pharaoh's invasion of Punt until the present; but no men, not even Cæsar's army of invasion in Britain, have had to land in an enemy's country with such a prospect of difficulty before them. They were going to land on a foodless cliff, five hundred miles from a store, in a place and at a season in which the sea's rising might cut them from supply. They had to take with them all things — munitions, guns, entrenching tools, sandbags, provisions, clothing, medical stores, hospital equipment, mules, horses, fodder, even water to drink, for the land produced not even that. These military supplies had to be arranged in boats and lighters in such a way that they might be thrust ashore with many thousands of men in all haste but without confusion. All this world of preparation, which made each unit landed a self-supporting army, took time and labour — how much can only be judged by those who have done similar work.

On Friday, the 23rd of April, the weather cleared so that the work could be begun. In fine weather in Mudros a haze of beauty comes upon the hills and water till their loveliness is unearthly, it is so rare. Then the bay is like a blue jewel, and the hills lose their savagery, and glow, and are gentle, and the sun comes up from Troy, and the peaks of Samothrace change colour, and all the marvellous ships in the harbour are transfigured. The land of Lemnos was beautiful with flowers at that season, in the brief Ægean spring, and to seawards always, in the bay, were the ships, more ships, perhaps, than any port of modern times has known; they seemed like half the ships of the world. In this crowd of shipping strange beautiful Greek vessels passed, under rigs of old time, with sheep and goats and fish for sale, and the tugs of the Thames and Mersey met again the ships they had towed of old, bearing a new freight, of human courage. The transports (all painted black) lay in tiers, well within the harbour, the men-of-war nearer Mudros and the entrance. Now in all that city of ships, so busy with passing picket-boats, and noisy with the labour of men, the getting of the anchors began. Ship after ship, crammed with soldiers, moved slowly out of harbour in the lovely day, and felt again the heave of the sea. No such gathering of fine ships has ever been seen upon this earth, and the beauty and the exultation of the youth upon them made them like sacred things as they moved away. All the thousands of men aboard them gathered on deck to see, till each rail was thronged. These men had come from all parts of the British world, from Africa, Australia, Canada, India, the Mother Country, New Zealand, and remote islands in the sea. They had said good-bye to home that they might offer their lives in the cause we stand for. In a few hours at most, as they well knew, perhaps a tenth of them would have looked their last on the sun, and be a part of foreign earth or dumb things that the tides push. Many of them would have disappeared for ever from the knowledge of man, blotted from the book of life none would know how — by a fall or chance shot in the darkness, in the blast of a shell, or alone, like a hurt beast, in some scrub or gully, far from comrades and the English speech and the English singing. And perhaps a third of them would be mangled, blinded or broken, lamed, made imbecile or disfigured, with the colour and the taste of life taken from them, so that they would never more move with comrades nor exult in the sun. And those not taken thus would be under the ground, sweating in the trench, carrying sandbags up the sap, dodging death and danger, without rest or food or drink, in the blazing sun or the frost of the Gallipoli night, till death seemed relaxation and a wound a luxury. But as they moved out these things were but the end they asked, the reward they had come for, the unseen cross upon the breast. All that they felt was a gladness of exultation that their young courage was to be used. They went like kings in a pageant to the imminent death. As they passed from moorings to the man-of-war anchorage on their way to the sea, their feeling that they had done with life and were going out to something new welled up in those battalions; they cheered and cheered till the harbour rang with cheering. As each ship crammed with soldiers drew near the battleships, the men swung their caps and cheered again, and the sailors answered, and the noise of cheering swelled, and the men in the ships not yet moving joined in, and the men ashore, till all the life in the harbour was giving thanks that it could go to death rejoicing. All was beautiful in that gladness of men about to die, but the most moving thing was the greatness of their generous hearts. As they passed the French ships, the memory of old quarrels healed, and the sense of what sacred France has done and endured in this great war, and the pride of having such men as the French for comrades, rose up in their warm souls, and they cheered the French ships more, even, than their own.

They left the harbour very, very slowly; this tumult of cheering lasted a long time; no one who heard it will ever forget it, or think of it unshaken. It broke the hearts of all there with pity and pride: it went beyond the guard of the English heart. Presently all were out, and the fleet stood across for Tenedos, and the sun went down with marvellous colour, lighting island after island and the Asian peaks, and those left behind in Mudros trimmed their lamps knowing that they had been for a little brought near to the heart of things.

The next day, the 24th of April, the troops of the landing parties went on board the warships and minesweepers which were to take them ashore. At midnight the fleet got under way from Tenedos and stood out for the Peninsula. Dawn was to be at five; the landings on the flanks were to take place then, the others at half-past five, after the fleet had bombarded the beaches. Very few of the soldiers of the landing parties slept that night; the excitement of the morrow kept them awake, as happened to Nelson's sailors before Trafalgar. It was a very still fine night, slightly hazy, with a sea so still that the ships had no trouble with their long tows of boats and launches. As it began to grow light the men went down into the boats, and the two flanking parties started for the outer beaches S and Y. The guns of the fleet now opened a heavy fire upon the Turkish positions, and the big guns on the Asian shore sent over a few shells in answer; but the Turks near the landing-places reserved their fire. During the intense bombardment by the fleet, when the ships were trembling like animals with the blasts of the explosions, the picket-boats towing the lighters went ahead, and the tow-loads of crowded men started for the main landings on beaches V, W, and X.

It was now light, and the haze on Sedd-el-Bahr was clearing away, so that those in charge of the boats could see what they were doing. Had they attempted an attack in the dark on those unsurveyed beaches among the fierce and dangerous tide rips, the loss of life would have been very great. As it was, the exceeding fierceness of the currents added much to the difficulty and danger of the task. We will take the landings in succession.

THE LANDING AT V BEACH, NEAR SEDD-EL-BAHR.

The men told off for this landing were: The Dublin Fusiliers, the Munster Fusiliers, half a battalion of the Hampshire Regiment, and the West Riding Field Company.

Three companies of the Dublin Fusiliers were to land from towed lighters, the rest of the party from a tramp steamer, the collier *River Clyde*. This ship, a conspicuous seamark at Cape Helles throughout the rest of the campaign, had been altered to carry and land troops. Great gangways or entry ports had been cut in her sides on the level of her between decks, and platforms had been built out upon her sides below these, so that men might run from her in a hurry. The plan was to beach her as near the shore as possible, and then drag or sweep the lighters, which she towed, into position between her and the shore, so as to make a kind of boat bridge from her to the beach. When the lighters were so moored as to make this bridge, the entry ports were to be opened, the waiting troops were to rush out on to the external platforms, run from them on to the lighters, and so to the shore. The ship's upper deck and bridge were protected with boiler plate and sandbags, and a casemate for machine guns was built upon her fo'c'sle, so that she might reply to the enemy's fire.

Five picket-boats, each towing five boats or launches full of men, steamed alongside the *River Clyde* and went ahead when she grounded. She took the ground rather to the right of the little beach, some four hundred yards from the ruins of Sedd-el-Bahr Castle, before the Turks had opened fire; but almost as she grounded, when the picket-boats with their tows were ahead of her, only twenty or thirty yards from the beach, every rifle and machine gun in the castle, the town above it, and in the curved, low, strongly trenched hill along the bay, began a murderous fire upon ship and boats. There was no question of their missing. They had their target on the front and both flanks at ranges between a hundred and three hundred yards in clear daylight, thirty boats bunched together and crammed with men and a good big ship. The first outbreak of fire made the bay as white as a rapid, for the Turks fired not less than ten thousand shots a minute for the first few minutes of that attack. Those not killed in the boats at the first discharge jumped overboard to wade or swim ashore. Many were killed in the water, many, who were wounded, were swept away and drowned; others, trying to swim in the fierce current, were drowned by the weight of their equipment. But some reached the shore, and these instantly doubled out to cut the wire entanglements, and were killed, or dashed for the cover of a bank of sand or raised beach which runs along the curve of the bay. Those very few who reached this cover were out of immediate danger, but they were only a handful. The boats were destroyed where they grounded.

Meanwhile the men of the *River Clyde* tried to make their bridge of boats by sweeping the lighters into position and mooring them between the ship and the shore. They were killed as they worked, but others took their places; the bridge was made, and some of the Munsters dashed along it from the ship and fell in heaps as they ran. As a second company followed, the moorings of the lighters broke or were shot; the men leaped into the water, and were drowned or killed, or reached the beach and were killed, or fell wounded there, and lay under fire, getting wound after wound till they died; very, very few reached the sandbank. More brave men jumped aboard the lighters to remake the bridge; they were swept away or shot to pieces. The average life on those boats was some three minutes long, but they remade the bridge, and the third company of the Munsters doubled down to death along it under a storm of shrapnel which scarcely a man survived. The big guns in Asia were now shelling the *River Clyde*, and the hell of rapid fire never paused. More men tried to land, headed by Brigadier-General Napier, who was instantly killed, with nearly all his followers. Then for long hours the remainder stayed on board, down below in the grounded steamer, while the shots beat on her plates with a rattling clang which never stopped. Her twelve machine guns fired back, killing any Turk who showed; but nothing could be done to support the few survivors of the landing, who now lay under cover of the sandbank on the other side of the beach. It was almost certain death to try to leave the ship, but all through the day men leaped from her (with leave or without it) to bring water or succour to the wounded on the boats or beach. A hundred brave men gave their lives thus; every man there earned the Cross that day. A boy earned it by one of the bravest deeds of the war, leaping into the sea with a rope in his teeth to try to secure a drifting lighter.

The day passed thus, but at nightfall the Turks' fire paused, and the men came ashore from the *River Clyde*, almost unharmed. They joined the survivors on the beach, and at once attacked the old fort and the village above it. These works were strongly held by the enemy. All had been ruined by the fire from the fleet, but in the rubble and ruin of old masonry there were thousands of hidden riflemen backed by machine guns. Again and again they beat off our attacks, for there was a bright moon and they knew the ground, and our men had to attack uphill over wire and broken earth and heaped stones in all the wreck and confusion and strangeness of war at night in a new place. Some of the Dublins and Munsters went astray in the ruins, and were wounded far from their fellows, and so lost. The Turks became more daring after dark; while the light lasted they were checked by the *River Clyde's* machine guns, but at midnight they gathered unobserved and charged. They came right down on to the beach, and in the darkness and moonlight much terrible and confused fighting followed. Many were bayoneted, many shot, there was wild firing and crying, and then the Turk attack melted away, and their machine guns began again. When day dawned, the survivors of the landing party were crouched under the shelter of the sandbank; they had had no rest; most of them had been fighting all night; all had landed across the corpses of their friends. No retreat was possible, nor was it dreamed of, but to stay there was hopeless. Lieut.-Colonel Doughty-Wylie gathered them together for an attack; the fleet opened a terrific fire upon the ruins of the fort and village, and the landing party went forward again, fighting from bush to bush and from stone to stone, till the ruins were in their hands. Shells still fell among them, single Turks, lurking under cover, sniped them and shot them; but the landing had been made good, and V beach was secured to us.

This was the worst and the bloodiest of all the landings.

THE LANDING AT W BEACH, UNDER CAPE TEKKE.

The men told off for this landing were the Ist Battalion Lancashire Fusiliers, supported (later) by the Worcester Regiment.

The men were landed at six in the morning from ships' boats run ashore by picket-boats. On landing, they rushed the wire entanglements, broke through them, with heavy loss, and won to the dead ground under the cliffs. The ships drew nearer to the beach and opened heavy fire upon the Turks, and the landing party stormed the cliffs and won the trenches.

The Worcester Regiment having landed, attempts were made to break a way to the right, so as to join hands with the men on V beach. All the land between the two beaches was heavily wired and so broken that it gave much cover to the enemy. Many brave Worcesters went out to cut the wires and were killed; the fire was intense, there was no getting farther. The trenches already won were secured and improved, the few available reserves were hurried up, and by dark, when the Turks attacked again and again, in great force, our men were able to beat them off, and hold on to what they had won.

THE LANDING AT X BEACH (SOMETIMES CALLED IMPLACABLE LANDING), TOWARDS KRITHIA.

The men told off for this landing were the Ist Royal Fusiliers, with a working-party of the Anson Battalion, R.N.D.

These men were towed ashore from H.M.S. *Implacable* about an hour after dawn. The ship stood close in to the beach, and opened rapid fire on the enemy trenches; under cover of this fire the men got ashore fairly easily. On moving inland, they were attacked by a great force of Turks and checked; but they made good the ground won, and opened up communications with the Lancashires who had landed at W beach. This landing was the least bloody of all.

Of the two flank landings, that on the right, within the Straits, to the right of Sedd-el-Bahr, got ashore without great loss and held on; that on the left, to the left of X beach, got ashore, fought a desperate and bloody battle against five times its strength, and finally had to re-embark. The men got ashore upon a cliff so steep that the Turks had not troubled to defend it; but on landing they were unable to link up with the men on X beach, as had been planned. They were attacked in great force by an ever-growing Turkish army, fought all day and all through the night in such trenches as they had been able to dig under fire, and at last in the morning of the next day went down the cliffs and re-embarked, most nobly covered to the end by a party from the King's Own Scottish Borderers and the Plymouth Battalion.

During the forenoon of the 25th, a regiment of the French Corps landed at Kum Kale, under cover of the guns of the French warships, and engaged the enemy throughout the day and night. Their progress was held up by a strongly entrenched force during the afternoon, and after sharp fighting all through the night they re-embarked in the forenoon of the 26th with some 400 Turkish prisoners. This landing of the French diverted from us on the 25th the fire of the howitzers emplaced on the Asiatic shore. Had these been free to fire upon us, the landings near Sedd-el-Bahr would have been made even more hazardous than they were.

At Bulair, one man, Lieutenant Freyberg, swam ashore from a destroyer towing a little raft of flares. Near the shore he lit two of these flares, then, wading on to the land, he lit others at intervals along the coast; then he wandered inland, naked, on a personal reconnaissance, and soon found a large Turkish army strongly entrenched. Modesty forbade further intrusion. He went back to the beach and swam off to his destroyer; could not find her in the dark, and swam for several miles, was exhausted and cramped, and was at last picked up, nearly dead. This magnificent act of courage and endurance, done by one unarmed man, kept a large Turkish army at Bulair during the critical hours of the landing. "The Constantinople papers were filled with accounts of the repulse of the great attack at Bulair." The flares deceived the Turks even more completely than had been hoped.

While these operations were securing our hold upon the extreme end of the Peninsula, the Australian and New Zealand Army Corps were making good their landing on the Ægean coast, to the north of Gaba Tepe. They sailed from Mudros on the 24th, arrived off the coast of the Peninsula at about half-past one on the morning of the 25th, and there under a setting moon, in calm weather, they went on board the boats which were to take them ashore. At about half-past three the tows left the ships, and proceeded in darkness to the coast.

Gaba or Kaba Tepe is a steep cliff or promontory about ninety feet high, with a whitish nose and something the look of a blunt-nosed torpedo or porpoise. It is a forbidding-looking snout of land, covered with scrub where it is not too steep for roots to hold, and washed by deep water. About a mile to the north of it there is a possible landing-place, and north of that again a long and narrow strip of beach between two little headlands. This latter beach cannot be seen from Gaba Tepe. The ground above these beaches is exceedingly steep sandy cliff, broken by two great gulleys or ravines, which run inland. All the ground, except in one patch in the southern ravine, where there is a sort of meadow of grass, is densely covered with scrub, mostly between two and three feet high. Inland from the beach, the land of the Peninsula rises in steep, broken hills and spurs, with clumps of pine upon them, and dense undergrowths of scrub. The men selected for this landing were the 3rd Brigade of the Australian and New Zealand Army Corps, followed and supported by the Ist and 2nd Brigades.

The place selected for the landing was the southern beach, the nearer of the two to Gaba Tepe. This, like the other landing-places near Cape Helles, was strongly defended, and most difficult of approach. Large forces of Turks were entrenched there, well prepared. But in the darkness of the early morning after the moon had set, the tows stood a little farther to the north than they should have done, perhaps because some high ground to their left made a convenient steering mark against the stars. They headed in towards the northern beach between the two little headlands, where the Turks were not expecting them. However, they were soon seen, and very heavy independent rifle fire was concentrated on them. As they neared the beach, "about one battalion of Turks" doubled along the land to intercept them. These men came from nearer Gaba Tepe, firing, as they ran, into the mass of the boats at short range. A great many men were killed in the boats, but the dead men's oars were taken by survivors, and the boats forced into the shingle. The men jumped out, waded ashore, charged the enemy with the bayonet, and broke the Turk attack to pieces. The Turks scattered and were pursued, and now the steep scrub-covered cliffs became the scene of the most desperate fighting.

The scattered Turks dropped into the scrub and disappeared. Hidden all over the rough cliffs, under every kind of cover, they sniped the beach or ambushed the little parties of the 3rd Brigade who had rushed the landing. All over the broken hills there were isolated fights to the death, men falling into gullies and being bayoneted; sudden duels, point blank, where men crawling through the scrub met each other, and life went to the quicker finger; heroic deaths, where some half-section which had lost touch were caught by ten times their strength and charged and died. No man of our side knew that cracked and fissured jungle. Men broke through it on to machine guns, or showed up on a crest and were blown to pieces, or leaped down from it into some sap or trench, to catch the bombs flung at them and hurl them at the thrower. Going as they did, up cliffs through scrub over ground which would have broken the alignment of the Tenth Legion, they passed many hidden Turks who were thus left to shoot them in the back or to fire down at the boats, from perhaps only fifty yards away. It was only just light, theirs was the first British survey of that wild country; only now, as it showed up clear, could they realize its difficulty. They pressed on up the hill; they dropped and fired and died; they drove the Turks back; they flung their packs away, wormed through the bush, and stalked the snipers from the flash. As they went, the words of their song supported them, the ribald and proud chorus of "Australia will be there" which the men on the torpedoed *Southland* sang as they fell in expecting death. Presently, as it grew lighter, the Turks' big howitzers began shelling the beach, and their field guns, well hidden, opened on the transports, now busy disembarking the 1st and 2nd Brigades. They forced the transports to stand farther out to sea, and shelled the tows, as they came in, with shrapnel and high explosive. As the boats drew near the shore, every gun on Gaba Tepe took them in flank, and the snipers concentrated on them from the shore. More and more Turks were coming up at the double to stop the attack up the hill. The fighting in the scrub grew fiercer; shells burst continually upon the beach, boats were sunk, men were killed in the water. The boatmen and beach working-parties were the unsung heroes of that landing. The boatmen came in with the tows, under fire, waited with them under intense and concentrated fire of every kind until they were unloaded, and then shoved off, and put slowly back for more, and then came back again. The beach parties were wading to and from that shell-smitten beach all day unloading, carrying ashore, and sorting the munitions and necessaries for many thousands of men. They worked in a strip of beach and sea some five hundred yards long by forty broad, and the fire directed on that strip was such that every box brought ashore had one or more shells and not less than fifty bullets directed at it

43

before it was flung upon the sand. More men came in and went on up the hill in support; but as yet there were no guns ashore, and the Turks' fire became intenser. By ten o'clock the Turks had had time to bring up enough men from their prepared positions to hold up the advance. Scattered parties of our men who had gone too far in the scrub were cut off and killed, for there was no thought of surrender in those marvellous young men; they were the flower of this world's manhood, and died as they had lived, owning no master on this earth. More and more Turks came up with big and field artillery, and now our attack had to hold on to what it had won, against more than twice its numbers. We had won a rough bow of ground, in which the beach represented the bowstring, the beach near Gaba Tepe the south end, and the hovel known as Fisherman's Hut the north. Against this position, held by at most 8,000 of our men, who had had no rest and had fought hard since dawn under every kind of fire in a savage rough country unknown to them, came an overwhelming army of Turks to drive them into the sea. For four hours the Turks attacked and again attacked, with a terrific fire of artillery and waves of men in succession. They came fresh from superior positions, with many guns, to break a disorganized line of breathless men not yet dug in. The guns of the ships opened on them, and the scattered units in the scrub rolled them back again and again by rifle and machine-gun fire, and by charge after counter-charge. More of the Army

Corps landed to meet the Turks, the fire upon the beach never slackened, and they came ashore across corpses and wrecked boats and a path like a road in hell with ruin and blasts and burning. They went up the cliff to their fellows under an ever-growing fire, that lit the scrub and burned the wounded and the dead. Darkness came, but there was no rest nor lull. Wave after wave of Turks came out of the night, crying the proclamation of their faith; others stole up in the dark through the scrub and shot or stabbed and crept back, or were seen and stalked and killed. Flares went up, to light with their blue and ghastly glare the wild glens peopled by the enemy. Men worked at the digging in till they dropped asleep upon the soil, and more Turks charged, and they woke and fired and again dug. It was cruelly cold after the sun had gone, but there was no chance of warmth or proper food; to dig in and beat back the Turk or die were all that men could think of. In the darkness, among the blasts of the shells, men scrambled up and down the pathless cliffs bringing up tins of water and boxes of cartridges, hauling up guns and shells, and bringing down the wounded. The beach was heaped with wounded, placed as close under the cliff as might be, in such yard or so of dead ground as the cliffs gave. The doctors worked among them and shells fell among them, and doctors and wounded were blown to pieces, and the survivors sang their song of "Australia will be there," and cheered the newcomers still landing on the beach. Sometimes our fire seemed to cease, and then the Turk shells filled the night with their scream and blast and the pattering of their fragments. With all the fury and the crying of the shells, and the shouts and cries and cursing on the beach, the rattle of the small arms and the cheers and defiance up the hill, and the roar of the great guns far away, at sea, or in the olive-groves, the night seemed in travail of a new age. All the blackness was shot with little spurts of fire, and streaks of fire, and malignant bursts of fire, and arcs and glows and crawling snakes of fire, and the moon rose, and looked down upon it all. In the fiercer hours of that night shells fell in that contested mile of ground and on the beach beyond it at the rate of one a second, and the air whimpered with passing bullets, or fluttered with the rush of the big shells, or struck the head of the passer like a moving wall with the shock of the explosion. All through the night the Turks attacked, and in the early hours their fire of shrapnel became so hellish that the Australians soon had not men enough left to hold the line. Orders were given to fall back to a shorter line, but in the darkness, uproar, and confusion, with many sections refusing to fall back, others falling back and losing touch, others losing their way in gully or precipice, and shrapnel hailing on all, as it had hailed for hours, the falling back was mistaken by some for an order to re-embark. Many men who had lost their officers and non-commissioned officers fell back to the beach, where the confusion of wounded men, boxes of stores, field dressing-stations, corpses, and the litter and the waste of battle, had already blocked the going. The shells bursting in this clutter made the beach, in the words of an eyewitness, "like bloody hell, and nothing else." But at this breaking of the wave of victory, this panting moment in the race, when some of the runners had lost their first wind, encouragement reached our men: a message came to the beach from Sir Ian Hamilton, to say that help was coming, and that an Australian submarine had entered the Narrows and had sunk a Turkish transport off Chanak.

This word of victory, coming to men who thought for the moment that their efforts had been made in vain, had the effect of a fresh brigade. The men rallied back up the hill; bearing the news to the firing-line, the new, constricted line was made good, and the rest of the night was never anything but continued victory to those weary ones in the scrub. But twenty-four hours of continual battle exhausts men, and by dawn the Turks, knowing the weariness of our men, resolved to beat them down into the sea. When the sun was well in our men's eyes they attacked again, with not less than twice our entire strength of fresh men, and with an overwhelming superiority in field artillery. Something in the Turk commander, and the knowledge that a success there would bring our men across the Peninsula within a day, made the Turks more desperate enemies there than elsewhere. They came at us with a determination which might have triumphed against other troops. As they came on they opened a terrific fire of shrapnel upon our position, pouring in such a hail that months afterwards one could see their round shrapnel bullets stuck in bare patches of ground, or in earth thrown up from the trenches, as thickly as plums in a pudding. Their multitudes of men pressed through the scrub as skirmishers, and sniped at every moving thing; for they were on higher ground, and could see over most of our position, and every man we had was under direct fire for hours of each day. As the attack developed, the promised help arrived; our warships stood in and opened on the Turks with every gun that would bear. Some kept down the guns of Gaba Tepe, others searched the line of the Turk advance, till the hills over which they came were swathed with yellow smoke and dust, the white clouds of shrapnel, and the drifting darkness of conflagration. All the scrub was in a blaze before them, but they pressed on, falling in heaps and lines; and their guns dropped a never-ceasing rain of shells on trenches, beach, and shipping. The landing of stores and ammunition never ceased during the battle. The work of the beach parties in that scene of burning and massacre was beyond all praise; so was the work of the fatigue parties, who passed up and down the hill with water, ammunition, and food, or dug sheltered roads to the trenches; so was the work of the Medical Service, who got the wounded out of cuts in the earth, so narrow and so twisted that there was no using a stretcher, and men had to be carried on stretcher-bearers' backs or on improvised chairs made out of packing-cases.

At a little before noon the Turk attack reached its height in a blaze and uproar of fire and the swaying forward of their multitudes. The guns of the warships swept them from flank to flank with every engine of death: they died by hundreds, and the attack withered as it came. Our men saw the enemy fade and slacken and halt; then with their cheer they charged him and beat him home, seized new ground from him, and dug themselves in in front of him. All through the day there was fighting up and down the line, partial attacks, and never-ceasing shell fire, but no other great attack: the Turks had suffered too much. At night their snipers came out in the scrub in multitudes and shot at anything they could see, and all night long their men dragged up field guns and piles of shrapnel, and worked at the trenches which were to contain ours. When day dawned, they opened with shrapnel upon the beach, with a *feu de barrage* designed to stop all landing of men and stores. They whipped the bay with shrapnel bullets. Where their fire was concentrated, the water was lashed as with hail all day long; but the boats passed through it, and men worked in it, building jetties for the boats to land at, using a big Turk shell as a pile-driver. When they got too hot they bathed in it, for no fire shook those men. It was said that when a big shell was coming men of other races would go into their dugouts, but that these men paused only to call it a bastard, and then went on with their work.

By the night of the second day the Australian and New Zealand Army Corps had won and fortified their position. Men writing or reporting on service about them referred to them as the A.N.Z.A.C., and these letters soon came to mean the place in which they were, unnamed till then, probably, save by some rough Turkish place-name, but now likely to be printed on all English maps, with the other names, of Brighton Beach and Hell Spit, which mark a great passage of arms.

CHAPTER
THREE

King Marsilies parted his army: ten columns
he kept by him, and the other ten rode in to
fight. The Franks said: "God, what ruin we
shall have here! What will become of the
twelve Peers?" The Archbishop Turpin answered
first: "Good knights, you are the friends of
God; to-day you will be crowned and
flowered, resting in the holy flowers of
Paradise, where no coward will ever come."
The Franks answered: "We will not fail. If it be
God's will, we will not murmur. We will fight
against our enemies; we are few men, but well
hardened."
They spurred forward to fight the pagans. The
Franks and Saracens are mingled.
— *The Song of Roland*.

This early fighting, which lasted from dawn on the
25th of April till noon on the following day, won us
a footing, not more than that, on the Peninsula; it
settled the German brag that we should never be
able to land. We had landed upon, had taken, and
were holding, the whole of the south-western

extremity of the Peninsula and a strip of the Ægean coast, in the face of an army never less than twice our strength, strongly entrenched and well supplied. We had lost very heavily in the attack, our men were weary from the exceedingly severe service of the landing, but the morrow began the second passage in the campaign, the advance from the sea, before the Turks should have recovered.

Many have said to me, with a naiveté that would be touching if it were not so plainly inspired by our enemies: "Why did not the troops press on at once the day they landed? The Japanese pressed on the day they landed, so did the Americans in Cuba. If you had pressed on at once, you would have won the whole Peninsula. The Turks were at their last cartridge, and would have surrendered."

It is quite true that the Japanese moved inland immediately from their transports at Chemulpho and Chinampo. Those ports were seized before the Russians knew that war was declared; they were not defended by Russian soldiers, and the two small Russian cruisers caught there by the Japanese fleet were put out of action before the transports discharged. The Japanese were free to land as they chose on beaches prepared, not with machine guns and mines, but with cranes, gangways, and good roads. Even so, they did not press on. The Japanese do not press on unless they are attacking; they are as prudent as they are brave; they waited till they were ready, and then marched on. The Americans landed at Daiquiri and at Guanica unopposed, and in neither case engaged the enemy till next day.

In the preceding chapter I have tried to show why we did not press on at once after landing. We did not because we could not, because two fresh men strongly entrenched, with machine guns, will stop one tired man with a rifle in nine cases out of ten. Our men had done the unimaginable in getting ashore at all; they could not do the impossible on the same day. I used to say this to draw the answer, "Well, other troops would have done it," so that I might say, what I know to be the truth, that no other men on this earth either would have or could have made good the landing; and that the men have not yet been born who could have advanced after such a feat of arms. The efforts of men are limited by their strength. The strength of men, always easily exhausted, is the only strength at the disposal of a General; it is the money to be spent by him in the purchase of victory, whether by hours of marching in the mud, digging in the field, or in attack. Losses in attack are great, though occasional; losses from other causes are great and constant. All armies in the field have to be supplied constantly with fresh drafts to make good the losses from attack and exhaustion. No armies can move without these replenishments, just as no individual man can go on working, after excessive labour, without rest and food. Our losses in the landings were severe, even for modern war, even for the Dardanelles. The bloodiest battle of modern times is said to have been the Antietam or Sharpsburg, in the American Civil War, where the losses were perhaps nearly one-third of the men engaged. At V beach the Munsters lost more than one-third, and the Dublins more than three-fifths, of their total strength. The Lancashires at W beach lost nearly as heavily as the Dublins. At Anzac, one Australian battalion lost 422 out of 900. At X beach, the Royals lost 487 out of 979. All these battalions had lost more than half their officers — indeed, by the 28th of April the Dublins had only one officer left. How could these dwindled battalions press on?

Then for the individual exhaustion. Those engaged in the first landing were clambering and fighting in great heat, without proper food, and in many cases without water, for the first twenty-four or thirty-six hours, varying the fighting with hurried but deep digging in marl or clay, getting no sleep, nor any moment's respite from the peril of death. Then, at the end of the first phase, when the fact that they had won the landing was plain, some of these same men, unrested, improperly fed, and wet through with rain, sweat, and the sea, had to hold what they had won, while the others went down to the beach to make piers, quarry roads, dig shelters, and wade out to carry or drag on shore food, drink, munitions, and heavy guns, and to do this without appliances, by the strength of their arms. Then, when these things had been done almost to the limit of human endurance, they carried water, food, and ammunition to the trenches, not in carts, but on their backs, and then relieved their fellows in the trenches, and withstood the Turk attacks and replied to the Turks' fire for hours on end. At Anzac, the A.N.Z. Army Corps had "ninety-six hours continuous fighting in the trenches, with little or no sleep," and "at no time during the ninety-six hours did the Turks' firing cease, although it varied in volume; at times the fusillade was simply deafening." Men worked like this, to the limit of physical endurance, under every possible exposure to wet, heat, cold, death, hunger, thirst, and want of rest, became exhausted, and their nerves shattered, not from fear, which was a thing those men did not understand, but because the machine breaks. On the top of the misery, exhaustion, and never-ceasing peril, is "the dreadful anxiety of not knowing how the battle is progressing," and the still worse anxiety of vigilance. To the strain of keeping awake, when dead-beat, is added the strain of watching men, peering for spies, stalking for snipers, and listening for bombing parties. Under all these strains the minds of strong men give way. They are the intensest strains ever put upon intelligences. Men subjected to them for many hours at a time cannot at once "press on," however brave their hearts may be. Those who are unjust enough to think that they can, or could, should work for a summer's day, without food or drink, at digging, then work for a night in the rain carrying heavy boxes, then dig for some hours longer, and at the end ask me to fire a machine gun at them while they "press on," across barbed wire, in what they presume to be the proper manner.

Our men could not "press on" at once. They had not enough unwounded men to do more than hold the hordes of fresh Turks continually brought up against them. They had no guns ashore to prepare an advance, nor enough rifle ammunition to stand a siege. They had the rations in their packs and the water in their bottles, and no other supplies but the seven days' food, water, and rifle ammunition put into each boat at the landing. To get men, stores, water, and guns ashore under fire, on beaches without wharves, cranes or derricks of any kind, takes time, and until men and goods were landed no advance was possible. Until then our task was not to press on, but to hang on, like grim death. It was for the enemy to press on, to beat our tired troops before their supports could be landed, and this the Turks very well understood, as their captured orders show, and as their behaviour showed only too clearly. During the days which followed the landing, the Turks, far from being at their last cartridge and eager to surrender, prevented our pressing on by pressing on themselves, in immense force and with a great artillery, till our men were dying of fatigue in driving back their attacks.

One point more may be discussed before resuming the story. The legend, "that the Turks were at their last cartridge, and would have surrendered had we advanced," is very widely spread abroad by German emissaries. It appears in many forms, in print, in the lecture, and in conversation. Sometimes place and date are given, sometimes the authority, all confidently, but always differently. It is well to state here the truth, so that the lie may be known. The Turks were never at the end of their supplies. They were always better and more certainly supplied with shells and cartridges than we were. If they were ever (as perhaps they sometimes were) rather short of big gun ammunition, so were we. If they were sometimes rather short of rifles and rifle ammunition, so were we. If they were often short of food and all-precious water, so were we, and more so, and doubly more so. For all our supplies came over hundreds of miles of stormy water infested by submarines, and were landed on open beaches under shell fire, and their supplies came along the Asiatic coast and by ferry across the Hellespont, and thence, in comparative safety, by road to the trenches. The Turkish army was well supplied, well equipped, more numerous, and in better positions than our own. There was neither talk nor thought among them at any time of surrender, nor could there have been in an army so placed and so valiant. There was some little disaffection among them. They hated their German officers and the German methods of discipline so much that many prisoners when taken expressed pleasure at being taken, spat at the name of German, and said, "English good, German bad." Some of this, however, may have been Levantine tact.

Late on the 26th of April, the French corps landed men at V beach, and took over the trenches on the right of the ground won — *i.e.*, towards the Straits. At noon the next day the whole force advanced inland, without much opposition, for rather more than a mile. At nightfall on the 27th, they held a line across the Peninsula from the mouth of the Sighir water-course (on the Ægean) to Eski Hissarlik (on the Straits). The men were very weary from the incessant digging of trenches, fighting, and dragging up of stores from the beach. They dug themselves in under shell and rifle fire, stood to their arms to repel Turk attacks for most of the night, and at eight next morning began the battle of the 28th of April. The French corps was on the right, the 29th Division (with one battalion of the R.N. Division) on the left. They advanced across rough moorland and little cultivated patches to attack the Turk town of Krithia. All the ground over which they advanced gave cover of the best kind to the defence. All through the morning, at odd times, the creeping companies going over that broken country came suddenly under the fire of machine guns, and lost men before they could fling themselves down. In the heather and torrent-beds of that Scotch-looking moorland, the Turk had only to wait in cover till his targets appeared, climbing a wall or getting out of a gully, then he could turn on his machine guns, at six hundred shots a minute each, and hold up the advance. From time to time the Turks attacked in great numbers. Early in the afternoon our advance reached its farthest point, about three-quarters of a mile from Krithia. Our artillery, short of ammunition at the best of times, and in these early days short of guns too, did what it could, though it had only shrapnel, which is of small service against an entrenched enemy. Those who were there have said that nothing depressed them more than the occasional shells from our guns in answer to the continual fire from the Turk artillery. They felt themselves out-gunned and without support. Rifle cartridges were running short, for, in spite of desperate efforts, in that roadless wild land with the beaches jammed with dead, wounded, stores, the wrecks of boats, and parties trying to build piers under shell fire, it was not possible to land or to send up cartridges in the quantity needed. There were not yet enough mules ashore to take the cartridge-boxes, and men could not be spared: there were too few men to hold the line. Gradually our men fell back a little from the ground they had won. The Turks brought up more men, charged us, and drove us back a little more, and were then themselves held. Our men dug themselves in as best they could and passed another anxious night, in bitter cold and driving rain, staving off a Turk attack, which was pressed with resolute courage against our centre and the French corps to the right of it. There were very heavy losses on both sides, but the Turks were killed in companies at every point of attack, and failed to drive us farther.

The next two days were passed in comparative

quiet, in strengthening the lines, landing men, guns, and stores, and preparing for the next advance. This war has shown what an immense reserve of shell is needed to prepare a modern advance. Our men never had that immense reserve, nor, indeed, a large reserve, and in those early days they had no reserve at all, but a day to day allowance, and before a reserve was formed the Turks came down upon us with every man and gun they had, in the desperate night attack of the 1st of May. This began with shell fire at 10p.m., and was followed half an hour later by a succession of charges in close order. The Turk front ranks crept up on hands and knees without firing (their cartridges had been taken from them), and charged our trenches with the bayonet. They got into our trenches in the dark, bayoneted the men in them, broke our line, got through to the second line, and were there mixed up in the night in a welter of killing and firing beyond description. The moon had not risen when the attack came home. The fighting took place in the dark: men fired and stabbed in all directions, at flashes, at shouts, by the burning of the flares, by the coloured lights of the Turk officers, and by the gleams of the shells on our right. There were 9,000 Turks in the first line, 12,000 more behind them. They advanced, yelling for God and Enver Pasha, amid the roar of every gun and rifle in range. They broke through, were held, then driven back, then came again, bore everything before them, and then met the British supports, and went no farther. Our supports charged the Turks and beat them back; at dawn our entire line advanced and beat them back in a rout, till their machine guns stopped us.

Upon many of the dead Turks in front of the French and English trenches were copies of an address issued by a German officer, one Von Zowenstern, calling on the Turks to destroy the enemy, since their only hope of salvation was to win the battle or die in the attempt. On some bodies were other orders, for the Mahometan priests to encourage the men to advance, for officers to shoot those soldiers who hung back, and for prisoners to be left with the reserves, not taken to the rear. In this early part of the campaign there were many German officers in the Turkish army. In these early night attacks they endeavoured to confuse our men by shouting orders to them in English. One, on the day of the landing, walked up to one of the trenches of the 29th Division, and cried out: "Surrender, you English, we ten to one." "He was thereupon hit on the head with a spade by a man who was improving his trench with it."

This battle never ceased for five days. The artillery was never silent. Our men were shelled, sniped, and shrapnelled every day and all day long, and at night the Turks attacked with the bayonet. By the evening of the 5th of May the 29th Division, which had won the end of the Peninsula, had been reduced by one-half and its officers by two-thirds. The proportion of officers to men in a British battalion is as one to thirty-seven, but in the list of killed the proportion was as one to eleven. The officers of that wonderful company poured out their lives like water; they brought their weary men forward hour after hour in all that sleepless ten days, and at the end led them on once more in the great attack of the 6th-8th of May.

This attack was designed to push the Allied lines farther forward into the Peninsula, so as to win a little more ground, and ease the growing congestion on the beaches near Cape Helles. The main Turkish position lay on and about the hump of Achi Baba, and on the high ground stretching down from it. It was hoped that even if Achi Baba could not be carried, the ground below him, including the village of Krithia, might be taken. The movement was to be a general advance, with the French on the right attacking the high ground nearer to the Straits, the 29th Division on the left, between the French and the sea, attacking the slowly sloping ground which leads past Krithia up to Achi Baba. Krithia stands high upon the slope, among orchards and gardens, and makes a good artillery target; but the slope on which it stands, being much broken, covered with dense scrub (some of it thorny) and with clumps of trees, is excellent for defence. The Turks had protected that square mile of ground with many machine guns and trenches so skilfully concealed that they could not be seen either from close in front or from aeroplanes. The French line of attack was over ground equally difficult, but steeper, and therefore giving more "dead ground," or patches upon which no direct fire can be turned by the defence. The line of battle from the French right to the English left stretched right across the Peninsula with a front (owing to bends and salients) of about five miles. It was nearly everywhere commanded by the guns of Achi Baba, and in certain places the enemy batteries on the Turk left, near the Straits, could enfilade it. Our men were weary, but the Turks were expecting strong reinforcements: the attack could not be delayed.

Few people who have not seen modern war can understand what it is like. They look at a map, which is a small flat surface, and find it difficult to believe that a body of men could have had difficulty in passing from one point upon it to another. They think that they themselves would have found no difficulty, that they would not have been weary nor thirsty, the distance demanded of them being only a mile, possibly a mile and a quarter, and the reward a very great one. They think that troops who failed to pass across that mile must have been in some way wanting, and that had *they* been there, either in command or in the attack, the results would have been different.

One can only answer, that in modern war it is not easy to carry a well-defended site by direct attack. In modern war you may not know, till fire breaks out upon you, where the defence, which you have to attack, is hidden. You may not know (in darkness, in a strange land) more than vaguely which is your "front," and you may pass by your enemy, or over him, or under him without seeing him. You may not see your enemy at all. You may fight for days and never see an enemy. In modern war troops see no enemy till he attacks them; then, in most cases if they are well entrenched with many guns behind them, they can destroy him.

The Allied officers, looking through their field-glasses at the ground to be attacked, could see only rough, sloping ground, much gullied, much overgrown, with a few clumps of trees, a few walls, orchards, and houses, but no guns, no trenches, no enemy. Aeroplanes scouting over the Turks could see men but not the trenches nor the guns; they could only report that they suspected them to be in such a place. Sometimes in the mornings men would notice that the earth was turned newly on some bare patch on the hill, but none could be sure that this digging was not a ruse to draw fire. The trenches were hidden cunningly, often with a head cover of planks so strewn with earth and planted with scrub as to be indistinguishable from the ground about. The big guns were coloured cunningly, like a bird or snake upon the ground. From above in an aeroplane an observer could not pick them out so as to be certain, if they were not in action at the time. Brave men scouting forward at night to reconnoitre brought back some information, but not more than enough to show that the Turks were there in force. No man in the Allied army expected less than a desperate battle; no officer in the world could have made it anything but that, with all the odds against us. Nothing could be done, but cover the Turk position with the fire of every gun on shore or in the ships, and then send the men forward, to creep or dash as far as they could go, and then dig themselves in.

Let the reader imagine himself to be facing three miles of any very rough broken sloping ground known to him, ground for the most part gorse-, thyme-, and scrub-covered, being poor soil, but in some places beautiful with flowers (especially "a spiked yellow flower with a whitish leaf"), and in others green from cultivation. Let him say to himself that he and an army of his friends are about to advance up the slope towards the top, and that as they will be advancing in a line along the whole length of the three miles, he will only see the advance of those comparatively near to him, since folds or dips in the ground will hide the others. Let him, before he advances, look earnestly along the line of the hill, as it shows up clear, in blazing sunlight, only a mile from him, to see his tactical objective, one little clump of pines three hundred yards away, across what seem to be fields. Let him see in the whole length of the hill no single human being — nothing but scrub, earth, a few scattered buildings of the Levantine type (dirty white with roofs of dirty red), and some patches of dark Scotch pine, growing, as the pine loves, on bleak crests. Let him imagine himself to be more weary than he has ever been in his life before, and dirtier than he has ever believed it possible to be, and parched with thirst, nervous, wild-eyed, and rather lousy. Let him think that he has not slept for more than a few minutes together for eleven days and nights, and that in all his waking hours he has been fighting for his life, often hand to hand in the dark with a fierce enemy, and that after each fight he has had to dig himself a hole in the ground, often with his hands, and then walk three or four roadless miles to bring up heavy boxes under fire. Let him think, too, that in all those eleven days he has never for an instant been out of the thunder of cannon, that waking or sleeping their devastating crash has been blasting the air across within a mile or two, and this from an artillery so terrible that each discharge beats, as it were, a wedge of shock between the skull-bone and the brain. Let him think, too, that never for an instant, in all that time, has he been free or even partly free from the peril of death in its most sudden and savage forms, and that hourly in all that time he has seen his friends blown to pieces at his side, or dismembered, or drowned, or driven mad, or stabbed, or sniped by some unseen stalker, or bombed in the dark sap with a handful of dynamite in a beef-tin, till their blood is caked upon his clothes and thick upon his face, and that he knows, as he stares at the hill, that in a few moments, more of that dwindling band, already too few, God knows how many too few, for the task to be done, will be gone the same way, and that he himself may reckon that he has done with life, tasted and spoken and loved his last, and that in a few minutes more he may be blasted dead, or lying bleeding in the scrub, with perhaps his face gone and a leg and an arm broken, unable to move but still alive, unable to drive away the flies or screen the ever-dropping rain, in a place where none will find him, or be able to help him — a place where he will die and rot and shrivel, till nothing is left of him but a few rags and a few remnants and a little identification disc flapping on his bones in the wind. Then let him hear the intermittent crash and rattle of the fire augment suddenly and awfully in a roaring, blasting roll, unspeakable and unthinkable, while the air above, that has long been whining and whistling, becomes filled with the scream of shells passing like great cats of death in the air; let him see the slope of the hill vanish in a few moments into the white, yellow, and black smokes of great explosions shot with fire, and watch the lines of white puffs marking the hill in streaks where the shrapnel searches a suspected trench; and then, in the height of the tumult, when his brain is shaking in his head, let him pull himself together with his friends, and clamber up out of the trench, to go forward against an invisible enemy, safe in some unseen trench expecting him.

The 29th Division went forward under these conditions on the 6th of May. They dashed on, or crawled, for a few yards at a time, then dropped for a few instants before squirming on again. In such an advance men do not see the battlefield. They see the world as the rabbit sees it, crouching on the ground, just their own little patch. On broken ground like that, full of dips and rises, men may be able to see nothing but perhaps the ridge of a bank ten feet ahead, with the dust flying in spouts all along it, as bullets hit it, some thousand a minute, and looking back or to their flanks they may see no one but perhaps a few men of their own platoon lying tense but expectant, ready for the sign to advance, while the bullets pipe over them in a never-ending bird-like croon. They may be shut off by some all-important foot of ground from seeing how they are fronting, and from all knowledge of what the next platoon is doing or suffering. It may be quite certain death to peep over that foot of ground in order to find out, and while they wait for a few instants, shells may burst in their midst and destroy a half of them. Then the rest, nerving themselves, rush up the ridge, and fall in a line dead under machine-gun fire.

The supports come up, creeping over their corpses, get past the ridge, into scrub which some shell has set on fire. Men fall wounded in the fire, and the cartridges in their bandoliers explode and slowly kill them. The survivors crawl through the scrub, half choked, and come out on a field full of flowers tangled three feet high with strong barbed wire. They wait for a while, to try to make out where the enemy is. They may see nothing but the slope of the field running up to a sky-line, and a flash of distant sea on a flank, but no sign of any enemy, only the crash of guns and the pipe and croon and spurt of bullets. Gathering themselves together, their brave men dash out to cut the wire, and are killed; others take their places, and are killed; others step out with too great a pride even to stoop, and pull up the supports of the wires and fling them down, and fall dead on top of them, having perhaps cleared a couple of yards. Then a couple of machine guns open on the survivors, and kill them all in thirty seconds, with the concentrated fire of a battalion.

The supports come up, and hear about the wire from some wounded man who has crawled back through the scrub. They send back word, "Held up by wire," and in time the message comes to the telephone which has just been blown to pieces by a shell. Presently, when the telephone is repaired, the message reaches the gunners, who fire high-explosive shells on to the wire, and on to the slopes where the machine guns may be hidden. Then the supports go on over the flowers, and are met midway by a concentrated fire of shells, shrapnel, machine guns, and rifles. Those who are not killed lie down among the flowers, and begin to scrape little heaps of earth with their hands to give protection to their heads. In the light sandy marl this does not take long, though many are blown to pieces or hit in the back as they scrape. As before, they cannot see how the rest of the attack is faring, nor even where the other platoons of the battalion are; they lie scraping in the roots of daffodils and lilies, while bullets sing and shriek a foot or two over their heads. A man peering from his place in the flowers may make out that the man next to him, some three yards away, is dead, and that the man beyond is praying, the man beyond him cursing, and the man beyond him out of his mind from nerves or thirst.

Long hours pass, but the air above them never ceases to cry like a live thing with bullets flying. Men are killed or maimed, and the wounded cry for water. Men get up to give them water, and are killed. Shells fall at regular intervals along the field. The waiting men count the seconds between the shells to check the precision of the battery's fire. Some of the bursts fling the blossoms and bulbs of flowers into the bodies of men, where they are found long afterwards by the X rays. Bursts and roars of fire on either flank tell of some intense moment in other parts of the line. Every feeling of terror and mental anguish and anxiety goes through the mind of each man there, and is put down by resolve.

The supports come up, they rise with a cheer, and get out of the accursed flowers, into a gully where some men of their regiment are already lying dead. There is a little wood to their front; they make for that, and suddenly come upon a deep and narrow Turk trench full of men. This is their first sight of the enemy. They leap down into the trench, and fight hand to hand, kill and are killed, in the long grave already dug. They take the trench, but opening from the trench are saps, which the Turks still hold. Men are shot dead at these saps by Turk sharpshooters cunningly screened within them.

Bullets fall in particular places in the trench from snipers hidden in the trees of the wood. The men send back for bombs; others try to find out where the rest of the battalion lies, or send word that from the noise of the fire there must be a battery of machine guns beyond the wood, if the guns would shell it.

Presently, before the bombs come, bombs begin to drop among them from the Turks. Creeping up, the men catch them in their hands before they explode, and fling them back so that they burst among the Turks. Some have their hands blown off, others their heads, in doing this, but the bloody game of catch goes on till no Turks are left in the sap, only a few wounded groaning men who slowly bleed to death there. After long hours the supports come up, and a storm of high explosives searches the little wood, and then with a cheer the remnant goes forward out of the trench into the darkness of the pines. Fire opens on them from snipers in the trees and from machine guns everywhere; they drop and die, and the survivors see no enemy, only their friends falling and a place where no living thing can pass. Men find themselves suddenly alone, with all their friends dead, and no enemy in sight, but the rush of bullets filling the air. They go back to the trench, not afraid, but in a kind of maze, and as they take stock and count their strength there comes the roar of the Turkish war-cry, the drum-like proclamation of the faith, and the Turks come at them with the bayonet. Then that lonely remnant of a platoon stands to it with rapid fire, and the machine gun rattles like a motor bicycle, and some ribald or silly song goes up, and the Turks fail to get home, but die or waver and retreat, and are themselves charged as they turn. It is evening now; the day has passed in long hours of deep experience, and the men have made two hundred yards. They send back for supports and orders, link up, if they are lucky, with some other part of their battalion, whose adventures, fifty yards away, have been as intense, but wholly different, and prepare the Turk trench for the night. Presently word reaches them from some far-away headquarters (some dug-out five hundred yards back, in what seems, by comparison, like peaceful England) that there are no supports, and that the orders are to hold the line at all costs and prepare for a fresh advance on the morrow. Darkness falls, and ammunition and water come up, and the stretcher-bearers hunt for the wounded by the groans, while the Turks search the entire field with shell to kill the supports which are not there. Some of the men in the trench creep out to their front, and are killed there as they fix a wire entanglement. The survivors make ready for the Turk attack, certain soon to come. There is no thought of sleep: it is too cold for sleep; the men shiver as they stare into the night. They take the coats of the dead, and try to get a little warmth. There is no moon, and the rain begins. The marl at the bottom of the trench is soon a sticky mud, and the one dry patch is continually being sniped. A few exhausted ones fall not into sleep, but into nervous dreams, full of twitches and cries, like dogs' nightmares, and away at sea some ship opens with her great guns at an unseen target up the hill. The terrific crashes shake the air; someone sees a movement in the grass and fires; others start up and fire. The whole irregular line starts up and fires, and machine guns rattle, the officers curse, and the guns behind, expecting an attack, send shells into the wood. Then slowly the fire drops and dies, and stray Turks, creeping up, fling bombs into the trench.

This kind of fighting, between isolated bodies of men advancing in a great concerted tactical movement stretching right across the Peninsula, went on throughout the 6th, the 7th, and the 8th of May, and ended on the evening of the 8th in a terrific onslaught of the whole line, covered by a great artillery. The final stage of the battle was a sight of stirring and awful beauty. The Allied line went forward steadily behind the moving barrier of the explosions of their shells. Every gun on both sides opened and maintained a fire dreadful to hear and see. Our men were fighting for a little patch of ground vital not so much to the success of the undertaking, the clearing of the Narrows, as to their existence on the Peninsula. In such a battle, each platoon, each section, each private soldier, influences the result, and "pays as current coin in that red purchase" as the Brigadier. The working-parties on the beaches left their work (it is said) to watch and cheer that last advance. It was a day of the unmatchable clear Ægean spring. Samothrace and Eubœa were stretched out in the sunset like giants watching the chess, waiting, it seemed, almost like human things, as they had waited for the fall of Troy and the bale-fires of Agamemnon. Those watchers saw the dotted order of our advance stretching across the Peninsula, moving slowly forward, and halting and withering away, among fields of flowers of spring and the young corn that would never come to harvest. They saw the hump of Achi Baba flicker and burn and roll up to heaven in a swathe of blackness, and multitudinous brightness changing the face of the earth, and the dots of our line still coming, still moving forward, and halting and withering away, but still moving up among the flashes and the darkness, more men, and yet more men, from the fields of sacred France, from the darkness of Senegal, from sheep-runs at the ends of the earth, from blue-gum forests, and sunny islands, places of horses and good fellows, from Irish pastures and glens, and from many a Scotch and English city and village and quiet farm; they went on and they went on, up ridges blazing with explosion into the darkness of death. Sometimes, as the light failed, and peak after peak that had been burning against the sky grew rigid as the colour faded, the darkness of the great blasts hid sections of the line; but when the darkness cleared they were still there, line after line of dots, still more, still

74

moving forward and halting and withering away, and others coming, and halting and withering away, and others following, as though those lines were not flesh and blood and breaking nerve, but some tide of the sea coming in waves that fell yet advanced, that broke a little farther, and gained some yard in breaking, and were then followed, and slowly grew, that halted and seemed to wither, and then gathered and went on, till night covered those moving dots, and the great slope was nothing but a blackness spangled with the flashes of awful fire.

What can be said of that advance? The French were on the right, the 29th Division on the left, some Australians and New Zealanders (brought down from Anzac) in support. It was their thirteenth day of continual battle, and who will ever write the story of even one half-hour of that thirteenth day? Who will ever know one-hundredth part of the deeds of heroism done in them, by platoons and sections and private soldiers, who offered their lives without a thought to help some other part of the line, who went out to cut wire, or brought up water and ammunition, or cheered on some bleeding remnant of a regiment, halting on that hill of death, and kept their faces to the shrapnel and the never-ceasing pelt of bullets as long as they had strength to go and light to see? They brought the line forward from a quarter of a mile to six hundred yards farther into the Peninsula; they dug in after dark on the line they had won, and for the next thirty-six hours they stood to arms to beat back the charges of the Turks, who felt themselves threatened at the heart.

Our army had won their hold upon the Peninsula. On the body of a dead Turk officer was a letter written the night before to his wife, a tender letter, filled mostly with personal matters. In it was the phrase, "These British are the finest fighters in the world. We have chosen the wrong friends."

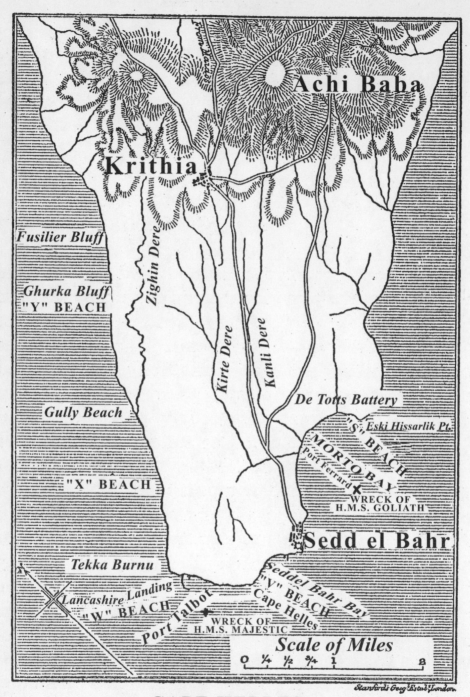

CAPE HELLES.

CHAPTER
FOUR

"So great is the heat that the dust rises."
— *The Song of Roland.*

During the next three weeks the Allied troops made small advances in parts of the lines held by them at Anzac and Cape Helles. Fighting was continuous in both zones; there was always much (and sometimes intense) artillery fire. The Turks frequently attacked in force, sometimes in very great force, but were repulsed. Our efforts were usually concentrated on some redoubt, stronghold, or salient, in the nearer Turkish lines, the fire from which galled our trenches or threatened any possible advance. These posts were either heavily bombarded and then rushed under the cover of a *feu de barrage*, or carried by surprise attack. Great skill and much dashing courage were shown in these assaults. The emplacements of machine guns were seized and the guns destroyed, dangerous trenches or parts of trenches were carried and filled in, and many roosts or hiding-places of snipers were made untenable. These operations were on a small scale, and were designed to improve the position then held by us, rather than to carry the whole line farther up the Peninsula. Sometimes they failed, but by far the greater number succeeded, so that by these methods, eked out by ruses, mines, clever invention, and the most dare-devil bravery, parts of our lines were advanced by more than a hundred yards.

On the 4th of June a second great attack was made by the Allied troops near Cape Helles. Like the attack of the 6th-8th May, it was an advance on the whole line, from the Straits to the sea, against the enemy's front-line trenches. As before, the French were on the right and the 29th Division on the left, but between them, in this advance, were the R.N. Division and the newly arrived 42nd Division. Our men advanced after a prolonged and terrible bombardment, which so broke down the Turk defence that the works were carried all along the line, except in one place, on the left of the French sector, and in one other place, on our own left, near the sea. Our advance, as before, varied in depth from a quarter of a mile to six hundred yards; all of it carried by a rush, in a short time, owing to the violence of the artillery preparation, though with heavy losses from shrapnel and machine-gun fire. In this attack the 42nd or East Lancashire Division received its baptism of fire. Even those who had seen the men of the 29th Division in the battles for the landing admitted that "nothing could have been finer" than the extreme gallantry of these newly landed men. The Manchester Brigade and two companies of the 5th Lancashire Fusiliers advanced with the most glorious and dashing courage, routed the Turks, and carried both their lines of trenches. One battalion, the 6th, very nearly carried the village of Krithia; there was, in fact, no entrenched line between them and the top of Achi Baba.

But in this campaign we were to taste, and be upon the brink of, victory in every battle, yet have the prize dashed from us, by some failure elsewhere, each time. So, in this first rush, when, for the first time, our men felt that they, not the Turks, were the real attackers, the victory was not to remain with us. We had no high-explosive shell and not enough shrapnel shell to deny to the Turks the use of their superior numbers and to hold them in a beaten state. They rallied and made strong counter-attacks, especially upon a redoubt or earthwork-fortress called the "Haricot," on the left of the French sector, which the French had stormed an hour before and garrisoned with Senegalese troops. The Turks heavily shelled this work and then rushed it. The Senegalese could not hold it; the French could not support it; and the Turks won it. Unfortunately the Haricot enfiladed the lines we had won. In a little while the Turks developed from it a deadly enfilade fire upon the R.N. Division, which had won the Turk trenches to the west of it. The R.N. Division was forced to fall back, and in doing so uncovered the right of the brigade of Manchesters beyond it to the westward. The Manchesters were forced to give ground, and the French were unable to make a new attack upon the Haricot, so that by nightfall our position was less good than it had been at half-past twelve.

But for the fall of the Haricot, the day would have been a notable victory for ourselves. Still, over three miles of the Allied front our lines had been pushed forward from two hundred to four hundred yards. This, in modern war, is a big advance, but it brings upon the conquerors a very severe labour of digging. The trenches won from the defence have to be converted to the uses of the attack and linked up, by saps and communication trenches, with the works from which the attack advanced. All this labour had to be done by our men in the midst of bitter fighting, for the Turks fought hard to win back these trenches in many bloody counter-attacks, and (as always happened after each advance) outlying works and trenches, from which fire could be brought to bear upon the newly won ground, had to be carried, filled in, or blown up before the new line was secure.

A little after dawn on the 21st of June the French stormed and won the Haricot redoubt, and advanced the right of the Allied position by six hundred yards. The Turkish counter-attacks were bloodily defeated.

In the forenoon of the 28th of June the English divisions advanced the left of the Allied position by a full one thousand yards. This attack, which was one of the most successful of the campaign, was the first of which it could be said that it was a victory. Of course our presence upon the Peninsula was in itself a victory, but in this battle we were not trying to land nor to secure ourselves, but (for the first time) to force a decision. Three of our divisions challenged the greater part of the Turk army and beat it. And here, for the first time in the operations, we felt, what all our soldiers had expected, that want of fresh men in reserve to make a success decisive, which afterwards lost us the campaign.

Our enemies have often said that the English cannot plan nor execute an attack. In this battle of the 28th of June the attack was a perfect piece of planning and execution. Everything was exactly timed, everything worked smoothly. Ten thousand soldiers, not one of whom had had more than six months' training, advanced uphill after an artillery preparation and won two lines of elaborately fortified trenches, by the bayonet alone. Then, while these men consolidated and made good the ground which they had won, the artillery lengthened their fuses and bombarded the ground beyond them. When the artillery ceased, ten thousand fresh soldiers climbed out of the English lines, ran forward, leaped across the two lines of Turk trench already taken, and took three more lines of trench, each line a fortress in itself. Besides advancing our position a thousand yards, this attack forced back the right of the Turks from the sea, and won a strong position between the sea and Krithia, almost turning Achi Baba. But much more than this was achieved. The great triumph of the day was the certainty then acquired that the Turks were beaten, that they were no longer the fierce and ardent fighters who had rushed V beach in the dark, but a shaken company who had caught the habit of defeat and might break at any moment. They were beaten; we had beaten them at every point, and they knew that they were beaten. Every man in the French and British lines knew that the Turks were at the breaking-point. We had only to strike while the iron was hot to end them.

As happened afterwards, after the battle of August, we could not strike while the iron was hot; we had not the men nor the munitions. Had the fifty thousand men who came there in July and August but been there in June, our men could have kept on striking. But they were not there in June, and our victory of the 28th could not be followed up. More than a month passed before it could be followed up. During that month the Turks dug themselves new fortresses, brought up new guns, made new stores of ammunition, and remade their army. Their beaten troops were withdrawn and replaced by the very pick and flower of the Turkish Empire. When we attacked again we found a very different enemy; the iron was cold, and we had to begin again from the beginning.

Thirty-six hours after our June success, at midnight in the night of June 29th-30th, the Turks made a counter-attack, not at Cape Helles, where their men were shaken, but at Anzac, where perhaps they felt our menace more acutely. A large army of Turks, about 30,000 strong, ordered by Enver Pasha "to drive the foreigners into the sea or never to look upon his face again," attacked the Anzac position under cover of the fire of a great artillery. They were utterly defeated, with the loss of about a quarter of their strength, some seven to eight thousand killed and wounded.

All this fighting proved clearly that the Turks, with all their power of fresh men, their closeness to their reserves, and their superior positions, could not beat us from what we had secured, nor keep us from securing more. Our advance into the Peninsula, though slow and paid for with much life, was sure and becoming less slow. What we had won we had fought hard for and never ceased to fight hard for, but we had won it and could hold it, and with increasing speed add to it; and the Turks knew this as well as we did. But early in May something happened which had a profound result upon the course of the operations. It is necessary to write of it at length, if only to show the reader that this Dardanelles Campaign was not a war in itself, but a part of a war involving most of Europe and half of Asia, and that that being so, it was affected by events in other parts of the war, as deeply as it affected those parts in turn by its own events.

No one of the many who spoke to me about the campaign knew or understood that the campaign, as planned, was not to be solely a French and English venture, but (in its later stages) a double attack upon the Turkish power, by ourselves on the Peninsula and the Hellespont, and by the Russians on the shores of the Black Sea. The double attack, threatening Turkey at the heart, was designed to force the Turks to divide their strength, and, by causing uneasiness among the citizens, to keep in and about Constantinople a large army which might otherwise wreck our Mesopotamian expedition, threaten India and Egypt, and prevent the Grand Duke Nicholas from advancing from the Caucasus on Erzerum. But as the Polish campaign developed adversely to Russia it became clear that it would be impossible for her to give the assistance she had hoped.

Early in May, Sir Ian Hamilton learned that his advance, instead of being a part of a concerted scheme, was to be the only attack upon the Turks in that quarter, and that he would have to withstand the greater part of the Turkish army. This did not mean that the Turks could mass an overwhelming strength against any part of his positions, since in the narrow Peninsula there is not room for great numbers to manœuvre; but it meant that the Turks would have always within easy distance great reserves of fresh men to take the place of those exhausted, and that without a correspondingly great reserve we had little chance of decisive success.

This change in the strategical scheme was made after we were committed to the venture; it made a profound difference to our position. Unfortunately we were so deeply engaged in other theatres that it was impossible to change our plans as swiftly and as profoundly as our chances. The great reserve could not be sent when it became necessary, early in May, nor for more than two months. Until it came, it happened, time after time, that even when we fought and beat back the Turks they could be reinforced before we could. All through the campaign we fought them and beat them back, but always, on the day after the battle, they had a division of fresh men to put in to the defence, while we, who had suffered more, being the attackers, had but a handful with which to follow up the success.

People have said: "But you could have kept fresh divisions in reserve as easily as the Turks. Why did you not send more men, so as to have them ready to follow up a success?" I could never answer this question. It is the vital question. The cry for "fifty thousand more men and plenty of high explosive" went up daily from every trench in Gallipoli, and we lost the campaign through not sending them in time. On the spot, of course, our Generals knew that war (like life) consists of a struggle with disadvantages, and their struggle with these was a memorable one. Only, when all was done, their situation remained that of the Frank rearguard in the "Song of Roland." In that poem the Franks could and did beat the Saracens, but the Saracens brought up another army before the Franks were reinforced. The Franks could and did beat that army, too, but the Saracens brought up another army before the Franks were reinforced. The Franks could and did beat that army, too, but then they were spent, and Roland had to sound his horn, and

Charlemagne would not come to the summons of the horn, and the heroes were abandoned in the dolorous pass.

Summer came upon Gallipoli with a blinding heat only comparable to New York in July. The flowers which had been so gay with beauty in the Helles fields in April soon wilted to stalks. The great slope of Cape Helles took on a savage and African look of desolation. The air quivered over the cracking land. In the blueness of the heat haze the graceful, terrible hills looked even more gentle and beautiful than before; and one who was there said that "there were little birds that droned, rather like the English yellow-hammers." With the heat, which was a new experience to all the young English soldiers there, came a plague of flies beyond all record and belief. Men ate and drank flies; the filthy insects were everywhere. The ground in places was so dark with them, that one could not be sure whether the patches were ground or flies. Our camps and trenches were kept clean; they were well scavenged daily. But only a few yards away were the Turk trenches, which were invariably filthy: there the flies bred undisturbed, perhaps encouraged. There is a fine modern poem which speaks of the Indian sun in summer as "the blazing death star." Men in Gallipoli in the summer of 1915 learned to curse the sun as an enemy more cruel than the Turk. With the sun and the plague of flies came the torment of thirst, one of the greatest torments which life has the power to inflict.

At Cape Helles, in the summer, there was a shortage, but no great scarcity, of water, for the Turk wells supplied more than half the army, and less than half the water needed had to be brought from abroad. At Anzac, however, there was always a scarcity, for even in the spring not more than a third of the water needed could be drawn from wells. At first water could be found by digging shallow pans in the beach, but this method failed when the heats began. Two-thirds (or more) of the water needed at Anzac had always to be brought from abroad, and to bring this two-thirds regularly and land it and store it under shell fire was a difficult task. "When operations were on," as in the August battle, the difficulty of distribution was added to the other difficulties, and then, indeed, want of water brought our troops to death's door. At Anzac, "when operations were on," even in the intensest heat the average ration of water for all purposes was, perhaps, at most, a pint and a half, sometimes only a pint. And though this extremity was as a rule only reached "when operations were on," that is, when there was heavy fighting, then the need was greatest.

In peace, in comfortable homes and in cool weather, civilized people need or consume a little less than three pints of liquid in each day. In hot weather and when doing severe bodily labour they need more, perhaps half a gallon in the day. Thirst, which most of us know solely as a pleasant zest to drinking, soon becomes a hardship, then, in an hour, an obsession, and by high noon a madness, to those who toil in the sun with nothing to drink. Possibly to most of the many thousands who were in the Peninsula last summer the real enemies were not the Turks, but the sun in heaven, shaking "the pestilence of his light," and thirst that withered the heart and cracked the tongue.

Some have said to me: "Yes, but the Turks must have suffered, too, just as much, in that waterless ground." It is not so. The Turks at Cape Helles held the wells at Krithia; inland fron Anzac they held the wells near Lonesome Pine and Koja Dere. They had other wells at Maidos and Gallipoli. They had always more water than we, and (what is more) the certainty of it. Most of them came from lands with little water and great heat, ten (or more) degrees farther to the south than any part of England. Heat and thirst were old enemies to them; they were tempered to them. Our men had to serve an apprenticeship to them, and pay for what they learned in bodily hardship. Not that our men minded hardship. They did not; they were volunteers who had chosen their fate and were there of their own choice, and no army in the world has ever faced suffering more cheerily. But this hardship of thirst was a weight upon them throughout the summer; like malaria, it did not kill, but it lowered all vitality. It halved the possible effort of men always too few for the work in hand. Let it now double the honour paid to them.

In the sandy soil of the Peninsula were many minute amœbæ, which played their part in the summer suffering. In the winds of the great droughts of July and August the dust blew about our positions like smoke from burning hills. It fell into food and water, and was eaten and drunk (like the flies) at each meal. Within the human body the amœbæ of the sand set up symptoms like those of dysentery, as a rule slightly less severe than the true dysentery of camps. After July nearly every man in our army in Gallipoli suffered from this evil. Like the thirst, it lowered more vitality than it destroyed. Many died, it is true, but then nearly all were ill; it was the universal sickness, not the occasional death, that mattered.

Pass now to the position of affairs at the end of June. We were left to our own strength in this struggle. The Turks were shaken; it was vital to our chances to attack again before they recovered. We had not the men to attack again, but they were coming, and were due in a few weeks' time. While they were on their way the question how to use them was considered.

As the army's task was to help the fleet through the Narrows, it had to operate in the south-western portion of the Peninsula. Further progress against Achi Baba in the Helles sector was hardly possible; for the Turks had added too greatly to their trenches there since the attacks of April and May. Operations on the Asian coast were hardly possible without a second army; operations against Bulair were not likely to help the fleet. Operations in the Anzac sector offered better chances of success. It was hoped that a thrust south-eastward from Anzac might bring our men across to the Narrows or to the top of the ridges which command the road to Constantinople. It was reasonable to think that such a thrust, backed up by a new landing in force to the north, in Suvla Bay, might turn the Turkish right and destroy it. If the men at Helles attacked, to contain the Turks in the south, and the men on the right of Anzac attacked, to hold the Turks at Anzac, it was possible that men on the left of Anzac, backed up by a new force marching from Suvla, might give a decisive blow. The Turk position on the Peninsula roughly formed a letter L. The plan (as it shaped) was to attack the horizontal line at Cape Helles, press the centre of the vertical line at Anzac, and bend back, crumple, and break the top of the vertical line between the Anzac position and Suvla. At the same time Suvla Bay was to be seized and prepared as a harbour at which supplies might be landed, even in the stormy season.

Some soldier has said, that "the simple thing is the difficult thing." The idea seems simple to us, because the difficulty has been cleared away for us by another person's hard thought. Such a scheme of battle, difficult to think out in the strain of holding on and under the temptation to go slowly, improving what was held, was also difficult to execute. Very few of the great battles of history, not even those in Russia, in Manchuria, and in the Virginian Wilderness have been fought on such difficult ground, under such difficult conditions.

The chosen battlefield (the south-western end of the Peninsula) has already been described; the greater part of it consists of the Cape Helles and Anzac positions, but the vital or decisive point, where, if all went well, the Turk right was to be bent back, broken and routed, lies to the north of Anzac, on the spurs and outlying bastions of Sari Bair.

Suvla Bay, where the new landing was to take place, lies three miles to the north of Anzac. It is a broad, rather shallow, semicircular bay, open to the west and south-west, with a partly practicable beach, some of it (the southern part) fairly flat and sandy, the rest steepish and rocky, though broken by creeks. Above it, one on the north, one on the south horn of the bay, rise two small low knolls or hillocks known as Ghazi Baba and Lala Baba, the latter a clearly marked tactical feature. To the north, beyond the horn of the bay, the coast is high, steep-to sandy cliff, broken with gullies and washed by deep water; but to the south, all the way to Anzac, the coast is a flat, narrow, almost straight sweep of sandy shore shutting a salt marsh and a couple of miles of lowland from the sea; it is a lagoon beach of the common type, with the usual feature of shallow water in the sea that washes it. The northern half of this beach is known as Beach C. the southern as Beach B.

Viewed from the sea, the coast chosen for the new landing seems comparatively flat and gentle, seemingly, though not really, easy to land upon, but with no good military position near it. It looks as though once, long ago, the sea had thrust far inland there, in a big bay or harbour stretching from the high ground to the north of Suvla to the left of the Anzac position. This bay, if it ever existed, must have been four miles long and four miles across, a very noble space of water, ringed by big, broken, precipitous hills, into which it thrust in innumerable creeks and combes. Then (possibly), in the course of ages, silt brought down by the torrents choked the bay, and pushed the sea farther and farther back, till nothing remained of the harbour but the existing Suvla Bay and the salt marsh (dry in summer). The hills ringing Suvla Bay and this flat or slightly rising expanse, which may once have been a part of it, stand (to the fancy) like a rank that has beaten back an attack. They are high and proud to the north; they stand in groups in the centre; but to the south, where they link on to the broken cliffs of the Anzac position, they are heaped in tumbling, precipitous, disordered bulges of hill, cut by every kind of cleft and crumpled into every kind of fold, as though the dry land had there been put to it to keep out the sea. These hills are the scene of the bitterest fighting of the battle.

Although these hills in the Suvla district stand in a rank, yet in the centre of the rank there are two gaps where the ancient harbour of our fancy thrusts creeks far inland. These gaps or creeks open a little to the south of the north and south limits of Suvla Bay. They are watered, cultivated valleys with roads or tracks in them. In the northern valley is a village of some sixty houses, called Anafarta Sagir, or Little Anafarta. In the southern valley is a rather larger village of some ninety houses, called Biyuk Anafarta, or Great Anafarta. The valleys are called after these villages.

Between these valleys is a big blunt-headed jut or promontory of higher ground, which thrusts out towards the bay. At the Suvla end of this jut, about one thousand yards from the bight of the Salt Marsh, it shoots up in three peaks or top-knots, two of them united in the lump called Chocolate Hill, the other known as Scimitar Hill or Hill 70; all, roughly, one hundred and fifty feet high. About a mile directly inland from Chocolate Hill is a peak of about twice the height, called Ismail Oglu Tepe, an abrupt and savage heap of cliff, dented with chasms, harshly scarped at the top, and covered with dense thorn scrub. This hill is the southernmost feature in the northern half of the battlefield. The valley of Great Anafarta, which runs east and west below it, cuts the battlefield in two.

The southern side of the Great Anafarta valley is just that disarrangement of precipitous bulged hill which rises and falls in crags, peaks, and gullies all the way from the valley to Anzac. Few parts of the earth can be more broken and disjointed than this mass of precipice, combes, and ravines. A savage climate has dealt with it since the beginning of time, with great heats, frosts, and torrents. It is not so much a ridge or chain of hills as the manifold outlying bastions and buttresses of Sari Bair, from which they are built out in craggy bulges parted by ravines. It may be said that Sari Bair begins at Gaba Tepe (to the south of the Anzac position), and stretches thence north-easterly towards Great Anafarta in a rolling and confused five miles of hill that has all the features of a mountain. It is not high. Its peaks range from about two hundred and fifty to six hundred feet; its chief peak (Koja Chemen Tepe) is a little more than nine hundred feet. Nearly all of it is trackless, waterless, and confused, densely covered with scrub (sometimes with forest), littered with rocks, an untamed savage country. The south-western half of it made the Anzac position; the north-eastern and higher half was the prize to be fought for.

It is the watershed of that part of the Peninsula. The gullies on its south side drain down to the Hellespont; those upon its north side drain to the flat land which may once have been submerged as a part of Suvla Bay. These northern gullies are great, savage, irregular gashes or glens running westerly or north-westerly from the hill bastions. Three of them, the three nearest to the northern end of the Anzac position, may be mentioned by name: Sazli Beit

Dere, Chailak Dere, and Aghyl Dere. The word Dere means watercourse; but all three were bone dry in August when the battle was fought. It must be remembered that in the trackless Peninsula a watercourse of this kind is the nearest approach to a road, and (to a military force) the nearest approach to a covered way. All these three Deres lead up the heart of the hills to those highlands of Sari Bair where we wished to plant ourselves. From the top of Sari Bair one can look down on the whole Turkish position facing Anzac, and see that position not only dominated, but turned and taken in reverse. One can see, only three miles away, the only road to Constantinople, and, five miles away, the little port of Maidos near the Narrows. To us the taking of Sari Bair meant the closing of that road to the passing of Turk reinforcements and the opening of the Narrows to the fleet. It meant victory, and the beginning of the end of this great war, with home and leisure for life again, and all that peace means. Knowing this, our soldiers made a great struggle for Sari Bair, but Fate turned the lot against them. Sari was not to be an English hill, though the flowers on her sides will grow out of English dust for ever. Those who lie there thought, as they fell, that over their bodies our race would pass to victory. It may be that their spirits linger there at this moment, waiting for the English bugles and the English singing, and the sound of the English ships passing up the Hellespont.

Among her tumble of hills, from the Anzac position to Great Anafarta, Sari Bair thrusts out several knolls, peaks, and commanding heights. Within the Anzac position is the little plateau of Lone or Lonesome Pine, to be described later. Farther to the north-east are the heights known as Baby 700 and Battleship Hill, and beyond these, still farther to the north-east, the steep peak of Chunuk Bair. All of these before this battle were held by the Turks, whose trenches defended them. Lone Pine is about four hundred feet high, the others rather more, slowly rising as they go north-east, but keeping to about the height of the English Chilterns. Chunuk Bair, the highest of these, is about seven hundred and fifty feet. Beyond Chunuk, half a mile farther to the north-east, is Hill Q, and beyond Hill Q a very steep, deep gully, above which rises the beautiful peak, the summit of Sari, known as Koja Chemen Tepe. One or two Irish hills in the wilder parts of Antrim are like this peak, though less fleeced with brush. In height, as I have said, it is a little more than nine hundred feet, or about the height of our Bredon Hill. One point about it may be noted. It thrusts out a great spur or claw for rather more than a mile due north; this spur, which is much gullied, is called Abd-el-Rahman Bair.

For the moment Chunuk Bair is the most important point to remember, because —

(*a*) It was the extreme right of the prepared Turk position.

(*b*) The three Deres previously mentioned have their sources at its foot and start there, like three roads starting from the walls of a city on their way to the sea. They lead past the hills known as Table Top and Rhododendron Spur. Close to their beginnings, at the foot of Chunuk, is a building known as the Farm, round which the fighting was very fierce.

The "idea" or purpose of the battle was "to endeavour to seize a position across the Gallipoli Peninsula from Gaba Tepe to Maidos, with a protected line of supply from Suvla Bay."

The plan of the attack was, that a strong force in Anzac should endeavour to throw back the right wing of the Turks, drive them south towards Kilid Bahr, and thus secure a position commanding the narrow part of the Peninsula.

Meanwhile a large body of troops should secure Suvla, and another large body, landing at Suvla, should clear away any Turkish forces on the hills between the Anafarta valleys, and then help the attacking force from Anzac by storming Sari Bair from the north and west.

The 6th of August was fixed for the first day of the attack from Anzac; the landing at Suvla was to take place during the dark hours of the night of the 6th-7th. "The 6th was both the earliest and the latest date possible for the battle — the earliest, because it was the first by which the main part of the reinforcements would be ready; the latest, because of the moon." Both in the preparation and the surprise of this attack dark nights were essential.

Sir Ian Hamilton's despatch (reprinted from the *London Gazette* of Tuesday, the 4th of January,

1916) shows that this battle of the 6th to 10th August was perhaps the strangest and most difficult battle ever planned by mortal General. It was to be a triple battle, fought by three separated armies, not in direct communication with each other. There was no place from which the battle, as a whole, could be controlled nearer than the island of Imbros (fourteen miles from any part of the Peninsula), to which telegraphic cables led from Anzac and Cape Helles. The left wing of our army, designed for the landing at Suvla, was not only not landed, when the battle began, but not concentrated. There was no adjacent subsidiary base big enough (or nearly big enough) to hold it. "On the day before the battle, part were at Imbros, part at Mudros, and part at Mitylene, . . . separated respectively by fourteen, sixty, and one hundred and twenty miles of sea from the arena into which they were simultaneously to appear." The vital part of the fight was to be fought by troops from Anzac. The Anzac position was an open book to every Turk aeroplane and every observer on Sari Bair. The reinforcements for this part of the battle had to be landed in the dark, some days before the battle, and kept hidden during daylight, so that the Turks should not see them and suspect what was being planned.

In all wars, but especially in modern wars, great tactical combinations have been betrayed by very little things. In war, as in life, the unusual thing, however little, betrays the unusual thing, however great. An odd bit of paper round some cigars betrayed the hopes of the American Secession; some litter in the sea told Nelson where the French fleet was; one man rising up in the grass by a roadside saved the wealth of Peru from the hands of Drake. The Turks were always expecting an attack from Anzac. It is not too much to say that they searched the Anzac position hourly for the certain signs of an attack, reinforcements, and supplies. They had not even to search the whole position for these signs, since there was only one place (towards Fisherman's Hut) where they could be put. If they had suspected that men and stores were being landed, they would have guessed at once that a thrust was to be made, and our attacks upon their flanks would have met with a prepared defence.

It was vital to our chance of success that nothing unusual, however little, should be visible in Anzac from the Turk positions during the days before the battle. One man staring up at an aeroplane would have been evidence enough to a quick observer that there was a newcomer on the scene. One new water-tank, one new gun, one mule not yet quiet from the shock of landing, might have betrayed all the adventure. Very nearly thirty thousand men, one whole division and one brigade of English soldiers, and a brigade of Gurkhas, with their guns and stores, had to be landed unobserved and hidden.

There was only one place in which they could be hidden, and that was under the ground. The Australians had to dig hiding-places for them before they came.

In this war of digging, the daily life in the trenches gives digging enough to every soldier. Men dig daily even if they do not fight. At Anzac in July the Australians had a double share of digging — their daily share in the front lines, and when that was finished their nightly share, preparing cover for the new troops. During the nights of the latter half of July the Australians at Anzac dug, roofed, and covered not less than twenty miles of dug-outs. All of this work was done in their sleep time, after the normal day's work of fighting, digging, and carrying up stores. Besides digging these hiding-places they carried up, fixed, hid, and filled the water-tanks which were to supply the newcomers.

On the night of the 3rd of August, when the landing of the new men began, the work was doubled. Everybody who could be spared from the front trenches went to the piers to help to land, carry inland, and hide the guns, stores, carts, and animals coming ashore. The nights, though lengthening, were still summer nights. There were seven hours of semi-darkness in which to cover up all traces of what came ashore. The newcomers landed at the rate of about 1,500 an hour, during the nights of the 3rd, 4th, and 5th of August. During those nights the Australians landed, carried inland, and hid, not less than one thousand tons of shells, cartridges, and food, some hundreds of horses and mules, many guns, and two or three hundred water-carts and ammunition-carts. All night long, for those three nights, the Australians worked like schoolboys. Often, towards dawn, it was a race against time, but always at dawn the night's tally of new troops were in their billets, the new stores were underground, and the new horses hidden. When the morning aeroplanes came over their observers saw nothing unusual in any part of Anzac. The half-naked men were going up and down the gullies, the wholly naked men were bathing in the sea; everything else was as it had always been, nor were any transports on the coast. For those three nights nearly all the Australians at Anzac gave up most of their sleep. They had begun the work by digging the cover; they took a personal pride and pleasure in playing the game of *cache-cache* to the end.

It is difficult to praise a feat of the kind, and still more difficult to make people understand what the work meant. Those smiling and glorious young giants thought little of it. They loved their chiefs and they liked the fun, and when praised for it looked away with a grin. The labour of the task can only be felt by those who have done hard manual work in hot climates. Digging is one of the hardest kinds of work, even when done in a garden with a fork. When done in a trench with a pick and shovel it is as hard work as threshing with a flail. Carrying heavy weights over uneven ground is harder work still; and to do either of these things on a salt-meat diet, with a scanty allowance of water, is very, very hard; but to do them at night, after a hard day's work, instead of sleeping, is hardest of all. Even farm-labourers would collapse and sailors mutiny when asked to do this last. It may be said that no one could have done this labour but splendid young men splendidly encouraged to do their best. Many of these same young men who had toiled thus almost without sleep for three days and nights fell in with the others and fought all through the battle.

But all this preparation was a setting of precedents and the doing of something new to war. Never before have 25,000 men been kept buried under an enemy's eye until the hour for the attack. Never before have two divisions of all arms been brought up punctually, by ship, over many miles of sea, from different ports, to land under fire, at an appointed time, to fulfil a great tactical scheme.

But all these difficulties were as nothing to the difficulty of making sure that the men fighting in the blinding heat of a Gallipoli August should have enough water to drink. Eighty tons of water a day does not seem very much. It had only to be brought five hundred miles, which does not seem very far, to those who in happy peace can telephone for eighty tons of anything to be sent five hundred miles to anywhere. But in war weight, distance, and time become terrible and tragic things, involving the lives of armies. The water-supply of that far battlefield, indifferent as it was at the best, was a triumph of resolve and skill unequalled yet in war. It is said that Wellington boasted that, while Napoleon could handle men, he, Wellington, could feed them. Our naval officers can truly say that, while Sir Ian

Hamilton can handle men, they can give them drink.

As to the enemy before the battle, it was estimated that (apart from the great strategical reserves within thirty or forty miles) there were 30,000 Turks in the vital part of the battlefield, to the north of Kilid Bahr. Twelve thousand of these were in the trenches opposite Anzac; most of the rest in the villages two or three miles to the south and south-east of Sari Bair. Three battalions were in the Anafarta villages, and one battalion was entrenched on Ismail Oglu Tepe; small outposts held the two Baba hillocks on the bay; and the land north of the bay was patrolled by mounted gendarmerie. These scattered troops on the Turk right had guns with them; it was not known how many. The beach of Suvla was known to be mined.

August began with calm weather. The scattered regiments of the divisions for Suvla, after some weeks of hard exercise ashore, were sent on board their transports. At a little before four o'clock on the afternoon of the 6th of August the 29th Division began the battle by an assault on the Turk positions below Krithia.

CHAPTER
FIVE

Roland put the horn to his mouth, gripped it hard, and with great heart blew it. The hills were high, and the sound went very far: thirty leagues wide they heard it echo. Charles heard it and all his comrades; so the King said: "Our men are fighting." Count Guenes answered: "If any other said that, I should call him a liar."

Count Roland, in pain and woe and great weakness, blew his horn. The bright blood was running from his mouth, and the temples of his brains were broken. But the noise of the horn was very great. Charles heard it as he was passing at the ports; Naimes heard it, the Franks listened to it. So the King said: "I hear the horn of Roland; he would never sound it if he were not fighting." Guenes answered: "There is no fighting. You are old and white and hoary. You are like a child when you say such things."

Count Roland's mouth was bleeding; the temples of his brain were broken. He blew his horn in weakness and pain. Charles heard it and his Franks heard it. So the King said: "That horn has long breath." Duke Naimes answered: "Roland is in trouble. He is fighting, on my conscience. Arm yourself. Cry your war-cry. Help the men of your house. You hear plainly that Roland is in trouble."

The Emperor made sound his horns . . . All the barons of the army mounted their chargers. But what use was that? They had delayed too long. What use was that? It was worth nothing; they had stayed too long; they could not be in time.

Then Roland said: "Here we shall receive martyrdom, and now I know well that we have but a moment to live. But may all be thieves who do not sell themselves dearly first. Strike, knights, with your bright swords; so change your deaths and lives, that sweet France be not ashamed by us. When Charles comes into this field he shall see such discipline upon the Saracens that he shall not fail to bless us."

— *The Song of Roland*.

The Cape Helles attack, designed to keep the Turks to the south of Kilid Bahr from reinforcing those near Anzac, became a very desperate struggle. The Turk trenches there were full of men, for the Turks had been preparing a strong attack upon ourselves, which we forestalled by a few hours. The severe fighting lasted for a week along the whole Cape Helles front, but it was especially bloody and terrible in the centre, in a vineyard to the west of the Krithia road. It has often happened in war that some stubbornness in attack or defence has roused the same quality in the opposer, till the honour of the armies seems pledged to the taking or holding of one patch of ground, perhaps not vital to the battle. It may be that in war one resolute soul can bind the excited minds of multitudes in a kind of bloody mesmerism; but these strange things are not studied as they should be. Near Krithia, the battle, which began as a containing attack, a minor part of a great scheme, became a furious week-long fight for this vineyard, a little patch of ground "two hundred yards long by a hundred yards broad."

From the 6th to 13th of August, the fight for this vineyard never ceased. Our Lancashire regiments won most of it at the first assault on the 6th. For the rest of the week they held it against all that the Turks could bring against them. It was not a battle in the military textbook sense: it was a fight man to man, between two enemies whose blood was up. It was a week-long cursing and killing scrimmage, the men lying down to fire and rising up to fight with the bayonet, literally all day long, day after day, the two sides within easy bombing distance all the time. The Turks lost some thousands of men in their attacks upon this vineyard; after a week of fighting they rushed it in a night attack, were soon bombed out of it, and then gave up the struggle for it. This bitter fighting not only kept the Turks at Cape Helles from reinforcing those at Anzac: it caused important Turk reinforcements to be sent to the Helles sector.

Less than an hour after the 29th Division began the containing battle at Krithia, the Australians at Anzac began theirs. This, the attack on the Turk fort at Lone Pine, in the southern half of the Anzac front, was designed to keep large bodies of Turks from reinforcing their right, on Sari Bair, where the decisive blow was to be struck. It was a secondary operation, not the main thrust, but it was in itself important, since to those at Anzac the hill of Lone Pine was the gate into the narrowest part of the Peninsula, and through that gate, as the Turks very well knew, a rush might be made from Anzac upon Maidos and the Narrows. Such a thrust from Lone Pine, turning all the Turkish works on the range of Sari Bair, was what the Turks expected and feared from us. They had shown us as much, quite plainly, all through the summer. Any movement, feint, or demonstration against Lone Pine brought up their reserves at once. It was the sensitive spot on their not too strong left wing. If we won through there, we had their main water-supply as an immediate prize, and no other position in front of us from which we could be held. Any strong attack there was therefore certain to contain fully half a division of the enemy.

The hill of Lone or Lonesome Pine is a little plateau less than four hundred feet high, running north-west by south-east, and measuring perhaps two hundred and fifty yards long by two hundred across. On its south-western side it drops down in gullies to a col or ridge, known as Pine Ridge, which gradually declines away to the low ground near Gaba Tepe. On its north-eastern side it joins the high ground known as Johnston's Jolly, which was, alas! neither jolly nor Johnston's, but a strong part of the Turk position.

We already held a little of the Lone Pine plateau. Our trenches bulged out into it in a convexity or salient known as the Pimple; but the Turks held the greater part, and their trenches curved out the other way, in a mouth, concavity, or trap opening towards the Pimple as though ready to swallow it. The opposing lines of trenches ran from north to south across the plateau, with from fifty to a hundred yards between them. Both to the north and south of the plateau are deep gullies. Just beyond these gullies Turk trenches were so placed that the machine guns in them could sweep the whole plateau. The space between the Australian and Turk lines was fairly level hill-top, covered with thyme and short scrub.

For some days before the 6th of August the warships had been shelling the Turk position on Lone Pine to knock away the barbed wire in front of it. On the 5th, the Australian brigade told off for the attack, sharpened bayonets, and prepared their distinguishing marks of white bands for the left arms and white patches for the backs of their right shoulders. In the afternoon of the 6th, the shelling by the ships became more intense; at half-past four it quickened to a very heavy fire; at exactly half-past five it stopped suddenly, "the three short whistle-blasts sounded and were taken up along the line, our men cleared the parapet" in two waves on a front of about one hundred and sixty yards, "and attacked with vigour." The hill-top over which they charged was in a night of smoke and dust from the explosions of the shells, and into that night, already singing with enemy bullets, the Australians disappeared. They had not gone twenty yards before all that dark and blazing hill-top was filled with explosion and flying missiles from every enemy gun. One speaks of a hail of bullets, but no hail is like fire, no hail is a form of death crying aloud a note of death, no hail screams as it strikes a stone, or stops a strong man in his stride. Across that kind of hail the Australians charged on Lone Pine. "It was a grim kind of steeplechase," said one, "but we meant to get to Koja Dere." They reached the crumpled wire of the entanglement, and got through it to the parapet of the Turk trench, where they were held up. Those behind them at the Pimple, peering through the darkness to see if any had survived the rush, saw figures on the parados of the enemy's trench, and wondered what was happening. They sent forward the third wave, with one full company carrying picks and shovels, to make good what was won. The men of this third wave found what was happening.

The Turkish front-line trench was not, like most trenches, an open ditch into which men could jump, but covered over along nearly all its length with blinders and beams of pinewood, heaped with sandbags, and in some places with a couple of feet of earth. Under this cover the Turks fired at our men through loopholes, often with their rifles touching their victims. Most of the Australians, after heaving in vain to get these blinders up, under a fire that grew hotter every instant, crossed them, got into the open communication trenches in the rear of the Turk line, and attacked through them; but some, working together, hove up a blinder or two, and down the gaps so made those brave men dropped themselves, to a bayonet fight like a rat fight in a sewer, with an enemy whom they could hardly see, in a narrow dark gash in the earth where they were, at first, as one to five or seven or ten.

More and more men dropped down or rushed in from the rear; the Turks, so penned in, fought hard, but could not beat back the attack. They surrendered, and were disarmed. The survivors were at least as many as their captors, who had too much to do at that time to send them to the rear, even if there had been a safe road by which to send them. They were jammed up there in the trenches with the Australians, packed man to man, suffering from their friends' fire and getting in the way.

The first thing to be done was to block up the communication trenches against the Turkish counter-attack. Every man carried a couple of sandbags, and with these breastworks and walls were built. Their work was done in a narrow, dark, sweltering tunnel, heaped with corpses and wounded, and crowded with prisoners who might at any moment have risen. Already the Turks had begun their counter-attacks. At every other moment a little rush of Turks came up the communication trenches, flung their bombs in the workers' faces, and were bayoneted as they threw. The trenches curved and zigzagged in the earth; the men in one section could neither see nor hear what the men in the nearest sections were doing. What went on under the ground there in the making good of those trenches will never be known. From half-past five till midnight every section of the line was searched by bombs and bullets, by stink-pots and sticks of dynamite, by gas-bombs and a falling tumult of shell and shrapnel, which only ceased to let some rush of Turks attack, with knives, grenades, and bayonets, hand to hand and body to body in a blackness like the darkness of a mine. At midnight the wounded were lying all over the trenches; the enemy dead were so thick that our men had to walk on them, and bombs were falling in such numbers that every foot in those galleries was stuck with human flesh. No man slept that night. At half-past seven next morning (the 7th) a small quantity of bread and tea was rushed across the plateau to the fighters, who had more than earned their breakfast. Turk shell had by this time blown up some of the head-cover, and some of the new communication trenches were still only a few feet deep. A Colonel, passing along one of them, told an officer that his section of the trench was too shallow. Half an hour later, in passing back, he found the officer and three men blown to pieces by a shell; in a few minutes more he was himself killed. At noon the bombing became so severe that some sections of the line were held only by one or two wounded men. At one o'clock the enemy attacked furiously with bomb and bayonet, in great force. They came on in a mass, in wave after wave, shoulder to shoulder, heads down, shouting the name of God. They rushed across the plateau, jumped into the trenches, and were mixed up with our men in a hand-to-hand fight, which lasted for five hours. Not many of them could join in the fight at one time, and not many of them went back to the Turk lines; but they killed many of our men, and when their last assault failed our prize was very weakly held. At half-past seven the survivors received a cheering (and truthful) message from the Brigadier, "that no fighters can surpass Australians," and almost with the message came another Turk assault, begun by bomb and shell and rifle fire, and followed by savage rushes with the bayonet, one of which got in, and did much slaughter. No man slept that night. The fight hardly slackened all through the night; at dawn the dead were lying three deep in every part of the line. Bombs fell every minute in some section of the line, and where the wide Turk trenches had been blasted open they were very destructive. The men were "extremely tired, but determined to hold on." They did hold on.

They held on for the next five days and nights, till Lone Pine was ours past question. For those five days and nights the fight for Lone Pine was one long personal scrimmage in the midst of explosion. For those five days and nights the Australians lived and ate and slept in that gallery of the mine of death, in a half-darkness lit by great glares, in filth, heat, and corpses, among rotting and dying and mutilated men, with death blasting at the doors only a few feet away, and intense and bloody fighting, hand to hand, with bombs, bayonets, and knives, for hours together by night and day. When the Turks gave up the struggle, the dead were five to the yard in that line of works; they were heaped in a kind of double wall all along the sides of the trench. Most of them were bodies of Turks, but among them were one-quarter of the total force which ran out from the Pimple on the evening of the 6th.

Like the fight for the vineyard near Krithia, this fight for Lone Pine kept large numbers of Turks from the vital part of the battlefield.

When the sun set upon this battle at Lone Pine on that first evening of the 6th of August, many thousands of brave men fell in for the main battle, which was to strew their glorious bodies in the chasms of the Sari Bair, where none but the crows would ever find them. They fell in at the appointed places in four columns, two to guard the flanks, two to attack. One attacking column, guarded and helped by the column on its right, was to move up the Chailak and Sazli Beit Deres to the storm of Chunuk Bair; the other attacking column, guarded and helped by the column on its left, was to move up the Aghyl Dere to the storm of Sari's peak of Koja Chemen Tepe. The outermost (left) guarding column (though it did not know it) was to link up with the force soon to land at Suvla.

They were going upon a night attack in a country known to be a wilderness, with neither water nor way in it. They had neither light nor guide, nor any exact knowledge of where the darkness would burst into a blaze from the Turk fire. Many armies have gone out into the darkness of a night adventure, but what army has gone out like this, from the hiding-places on a beach to the heart of unknown hills, to wander up crags under fire, to storm a fortress in the dawn? Even in Manchuria there were roads and the traces and the comforts of man. In this savagery there was nothing but the certainty of desolation, where the wounded would lie until they died and the dead be never buried.

Until this campaign the storm of Badajos was the most desperate duty ever given to British soldiers. The men in the forlorn hope of that storm marched to their position to the sound of fifes, "which filled the heart with a melting sweetness," and tuned that rough company to a kind of sacred devotion. No music played away the brave men from Anzac. They answered to their names in the dark, and moved off to take position for what they had to do. Men of many races were banded together there. There were Australians, English, Indians, Maoris and New Zealanders, made one by devotion to a cause, and all willing to die that so their comrades might see the dawn make a steel streak of the Hellespont from the peaked hill now black against the stars. Soon they had turned their backs on friendly little Anzac and the lights in the gullies, and were stepping out with the sea upon their left and the hills of their destiny upon their right, and the shells, star-lights, and battle of Lone Pine far away behind them. Before 9p.m. the right covering column (of New Zealanders) was in position, ready to open up the Sazli Beit and Chailak Deres to their brothers, who were to storm Chunuk. Half an hour later, cunningly backed by the guns of the destroyer *Colne*, they rushed the Turk position, routed the garrison and its supports, and took the fort known as Old No. 3 Post. It was an immensely strong position, protected by barbed wire, shielded by shell-proof head-cover, and mined in front "with twenty-eight mines electrically connected to a first-rate firing apparatus within." *Sed nisi Dominus.*

This success opened up the Sazli Dere for nearly half of its length.

Inland from Old No. 3 Post, and some seven hundred yards from it, is a crag or precipice which looks like a round table, with a top projecting beyond its legs. This crag, known to our men as Table-Top, is a hill which few would climb for pleasure. Nearly all the last one hundred feet of the peak is precipice, such as no mountaineer would willingly climb without clear daylight and every possible precaution. It is a sort of skull of rock fallen down upon its body of rock, and the great rocky

117

ribs heave out with gullies between them. The Table-Top, or plateau summit, was strongly entrenched and held by the Turks, whose communication trenches ran down the back of the hill to Rhododendron Spur.

While their comrades were rushing Old No. 3 Post, a party of New Zealanders marched to storm this natural fortress. The muscular part of the feat may be likened to the climbing of the Welsh Glyddyrs, the Irish Lurig, or the craggier parts of the American Palisades, in a moonless midnight, under a load of not less than thirty pounds. But the muscular effort was made much greater by the roughness of the unknown approaches, which led over glidders of loose stones into the densest of short, thick, intensely thorny scrub. The New Zealanders advanced under fire through this scrub, went up the rocks in a spirit which no crag could daunt, reached the Table-Top, rushed the Turk trenches, killed some Turks of the garrison, and captured the rest with all their stores.

This success opened up the remainder of the Sazli Beit Dere.

While these attacks were progressing, the remainder of the right covering column marched north to the Chailak Dere. A large body crossed this Dere and marched on, but the rest turned up the Dere, and soon came to a barbed-wire entanglement which blocked the ravine. They had met the Turks' barbed wire before, on Anzac Day, and had won through it; but this wire in the Dere was new to their experience: it was meant rather as a permanent work than as an obstruction. It was secured to great balks or blinders of pine, six or eight feet high, which stood in a rank twenty or thirty deep right across the ravinc. The wire, which crossed and criss-crossed between these balks, was as thick as a man's thumb and profusely barbed. Beyond it lay a flanking trench, held by a strong outpost of Turks, who at once opened fire. This, though not unexpected, was a difficult barrier to come upon in the darkness of a summer night, and here, as before, at the landing of the Worcester Regiment at W beach, men went forward quietly, without weapons, to cut the wire for the others. They were shot down, but others took their places, though the Turks, thirty steps away on the other side of the gully, had only to hold their rifles steady and pull their triggers to destroy them. This holding up in the darkness by an unseen hidden enemy and an obstacle which needed high-explosive shell in quantity caused heavy loss and great delay. For a time there was no getting through; but then, with the most desperate courage and devotion, a party of Engineers cleared the obstacle, the Turks were routed, and a path made for the attackers.

This success opened up the mouth of the Chailak Dere.

Meanwhile those who had marched across this Dere and gone on towards Suvla swung round to the right to clear the Turks from Bauchop's Hill, which overlooks the Chailak Dere from the north.

119

Bauchop's Hill (a rough country even for Gallipoli) is cleft by not less than twenty great gullies, most of them forked, precipitous, overgrown, and heaped with rocks. The New Zealanders scrambled up it from the north, got into a maze of trenches, not strongly held, beat the Turks out of them, wandered south across the neck or ridge of the hill, discovering Turk trenches by their fire, and at last secured the whole hill.

This success, besides securing the Chailak Dere from any assault from the north, secured the south flank of the Aghyl Dere beyond it.

Meanwhile the left covering column (mainly Welshmen), which for some time had halted at Old No. 3 Post, waiting for the sound of battle to tell them that the Turks on Bauchop's Hill were engaged, marched boldly on the Aghyl Dere, crossed it in a rush, taking every Turk trench in the way, then stormed the Turk outpost on Damakjelik Bair, going on from trench to trench in the dark, guided by the flashes of the rifles, till the whole hill was theirs. This success opened up the Aghyl Dere to the attacking column.

As the troops drew their breath in the still night on the little hill which they had won, they heard about three miles away a noise of battle on the sea coast to their left. This noise was not the nightly "hate" of the monitors and destroyers, but an irregular and growing rifle fire. This, though they did not know it, was the beginning of the landing of the new divisions, with their 30,000 men, at Suvla Bay.

For the moment, Suvla was not the important point in the battle. The three Deres were the important points, for up the three Deres, now cleared of Turks, our attacking columns were advancing to the assault.

By this time, however, the Turks were roused throughout their line. All the Anzac position from Tasmania Post to Table-Top was a blaze of battle to contain them before our trenches; but they knew now that their right was threatened, and their reserves were hurrying out to meet us before we had gained the crests. Our right attacking column (of English and New Zealand troops) went up the Sazli Beit and Chailak Deres, deployed beyond Table-Top, and stormed Rhododendron Spur, fighting for their lives every inch of the way. The left column (mainly Indians and Australians) pressed up the Aghyl, into the stony clefts of its upper forks, and so, by rock, jungle, heart-breaking cliff and fissure, to the attack of Hill Q and the lower slopes of Sari. They, too, were fighting for their lives. Their advance was across a scrub peopled now by little clumps of marksmen firing from hiding. When they deployed out of the Deres, to take up their line of battle, they linked up with the right assaulting column, and formed with them a front of about a mile, stretching from the old Anzac position to within a mile of the crests which were the prize. By this time the night was over, day was breaking, the

Turks were in force, and our attacking columns much exhausted, but there was still breath for a last effort. Now, with the breath, came a quick encouragement, for looking down from their hillsides, they could see Suvla Bay full of ships, the moving marks of boats, dotted specks of men on the sandhills, and more ships on the sea marching like chariots to the cannon. In a flash, as happens when many minds are tense together, they realized the truth. A new landing was being made. All along the coast by the Bay the crackle and the flash of firing was moving from the sea, to show them that the landing was made good, and that the Turks were falling back. Hardening their hearts at this sight of help coming from the sea, the Australians and Sikhs, with the last of their strength, went at Koja Chemen Tepe, and the New Zealanders upon their right rose to the storm of Chunuk.

It was not to be. The guns behind them backed them. They did what mortal men could do, but they were worn out by the night's advance; they could not carry the two summits. They tried a second time to carry Chunuk; but they were too weary and the Turks in too great strength: they could not get to the top. But they held to what they had won; they entrenched themselves on the new line, and there they stayed, making ready for the next attack.

Two or three have said to me: "They ought not to have been exhausted; none of them had marched five miles." It is difficult to answer such critics patiently, doubly difficult to persuade them, without showing them the five miles. There comes into my mind, as I write, the image of some hills in the West of Ireland, a graceful and austere range, not difficult to climb, seemingly, and not unlike these Gallipoli hills, in their look of lying down at rest. The way to those hills is over some miles of scattered limestone blocks, with gaps between them full of scrub, gorse, heather, dwarf-ash, and little hill-thorn, and the traveller proceeds, as the devil went through Athlone, "in standing lepps." This journey to the hills is the likest journey (known to me) to that of the assaulting columns. Like the devil in Athlone, the assaulting columns had often to advance "in standing lepps," but to them the standing lepp came as a solace, a rare, strange, and blessed respite, from forcing through scrub by main strength, or scaling a crag of rotten sandstone, in pitch darkness, in the presence of an enemy. For an armed force to advance a mile an hour by day over such a country is not only good going, but a great achievement; to advance four miles in a night over such a country, fighting literally all the way, often hand to hand, and to feel the enemy's resistance stiffening and his reserves arriving as the strength fails and the ascent steepens, and yet to make an effort at the end, is a thing unknown in the history of war. And this first fourteen hours of exhausting physical labour was but the beginning. The troops, as they very well knew, were to have two or three days more of the same toil before the battle could be ended, one way or the other. So after struggling for fourteen hours with every muscle in their bodies, over crags and down gullies in the never-ceasing peril of death, they halted in the blaze of noon and drew their breath. In the evening, as they hoped, the men from Suvla would join hands and go on to victory with them; they had fought the first stage of the battle, the next stage was to be decisive.

The heat of this noon of the 7th of August on those sandy hills was a scarcely bearable torment.

Meanwhile at Suvla, the left of the battle, the 11th Division had landed in the pitch darkness, by wading ashore, in five feet of water, under rifle fire, on to beaches prepared with land mines. The first boat-loads lost many men from the mines and from the fire of snipers, who came right down to the beach in the darkness, and fired from the midst of our men. These snipers were soon bayoneted; our men formed for the assault in the dark, and stormed the Turk outpost on Lala Baba there and then. While Lala Baba was being cleared, other battalions moved north to clear the Turks from the neighbourhood of the beach on that side. The ground over which they had to move is a sand-dune land, covered with gorse and other scrub, most difficult to advance across in a wide extension. About half a mile from the beach the ground rises in a roll or whale-back, known on the battle plans as Hill 10. This hill is about three hundred yards long and thirty feet high. At this whale-back (which was entrenched) the Turks rallied on their supports; they had, perhaps, a couple of thousand men and (some say) a gun or two, and the dawn broke before they could be rushed. Their first shells upon our men set fire to the gorse, so that our advance against them was through a blazing common, in which many men who fell wounded were burnt to death or suffocated. The Turks, seeing the difficulties of the men in the fire, charged with the bayonet, but were themselves charged and driven back in great disorder; the fire spread to their hill, and burned them out of it. Our men then began to drive the Turks away from the high ridges to the north of Suvla. The 10th Division began to land while this fight was still in progress.

This early fighting had won for us a landing-place at Suvla, and had cleared the ground to the north of the Bay for the deployment for the next attack. This was to be a swinging round of two brigades to the storm of the hills directly to the east of the Salt Lake. These hills are the island-like, double-peaked Chocolate Hill (close to the Lake), and the much higher and more important hills of Scimitar Hill (or Hill 70) and Ismail Oglu Tepe (Hill 100) behind it. The brigade chosen for this attack were the 31st (consisting of Irish Regiments), and the 32nd (consisting of Yorkshire and North of England Regiments), belonging to the 11th Division. The 32nd had been hotly engaged since the very early morning, the 31st were only just on shore. The storm was to be pushed from the north, and would, if successful, clear the way for the final thrust, the storm of Koja Chemen Tepe from the north-west.

This thrust from Suvla against Koja Chemen was designed to complete and make decisive the thrust already begun by the right and left attacking columns. The attack on Chocolate Hill, Scimitar Hill, and Ismail Oglu, was to make that thrust possible by destroying for ever the power of the Turk to parry it. The Turk could only parry it by firing from those hills on the men making it. It was therefore necessary to seize those hills before the Turk could stop us. If the Turks seized those hills before us, or stopped us from seizing them, our troops could not march from Suvla to take part in the storm of Koja Chemen. If we seized them before the Turks, then the Turks could not stop us from crossing the valley to that storm. The first problem at Suvla, therefore, was not so much to win a battle as to win a race with the Turks for the possession of those hills; the winning of the battle could be arranged later. Our failure to win that race brought with it our loss of the battle. The next chapter in the story of the battle is simply a description of the losing of a race by loss of time.

Now the giving of praise or blame is always easy, but the understanding of anything is difficult. The understanding of anything so vast, so confused, so full of contradiction, so dependent on little things (themselves changing from minute to minute, the coward of a moment ago blazing out into a hero at the next turn) as a modern battle, is more than difficult. But some attempt must be made to understand how it came about that time was lost at Suvla between the landing, at midnight, on the 6th-7th of August, and the arrival of the Turks upon the hills, at midnight, on the 8th-9th.

In the first place, it should be said that the beaches of Suvla are not the beaches of seaside resorts, all pleasant, smooth sand and shingle. They are called beaches because they cannot well be called cliffs. They slope into the sea with some abruptness, in *pentes* of rock and tumbles of sand-dune difficult to land upon from boats. From them one climbs on to sand-dune into a sand-dune land, which is like nothing so much as a sea-marsh from which the water has receded. Walking on this soft sand is difficult: it is like walking in feathers; working, hauling, and carrying upon it is very difficult. Upon this coast and country, roadless, wharfless, beachless and unimproved, nearly 30,000 men landed in the first ten hours of the 7th of August. At 10a.m. on that day, when the sun was in his stride, the difficulty of those beaches began to tell on those upon them. There had been sharp fighting on and near the beaches, and shells were still falling here and there in all the ground which we had won. On and near the beaches there was a congestion of a very hindering kind. With men coming ashore, shells bursting among them; mules landing, biting, kicking, shying, and stampeding; guns limbering up and trying to get out into position; more men coming ashore or seeking for

127

the rest of their battalion in a crowd where all battalions looked alike; shouts, orders, and counter-orders; ammunition boxes being passed along; water-carts and transport being started for the firing-line; wounded coming down, or being helped down, or being loaded into lighters; doctors trying to clear the way for field dressing-stations, with every now and then a shell from Ismail sending the sand in clouds over corpses, wounded men, and fatigue parties; and a blinding August sun over all to exhaust and to madden: it was not possible to avoid congestion. This congestion was the first, but not the most fatal, cause of the loss of time.

Though the congestion was an evil in itself, its first evil effect was that it made it impossible to pass orders quickly from one part of the beach to another. In this first matter of the attack on the hills, the way had been opened for the assault by 10a.m. at the latest; but to get through the confusion along the beaches (among battalions landing, forming, and defiling, and the waste of wounded momently increasing), to arrange for the assault and to pass the orders to the battalions named for the duty, took a great deal of time. It was nearly 1p.m. when the 31st moved north from Lala Baba on their march round the head of the Salt Lake into position for the attack. The 32nd Brigade, having fought since dawn at Hill 10, was already to the north of the Salt Lake; but when (at about 3p.m.) the 31st took position, facing south-east, with its right on the north-east corner of the Salt Lake, the 32nd was not upon its left ready to advance with it. Instead of that guard upon its left the 31st found a vigorous attack of Turks. More time was lost waiting for support to reach the left, and before it arrived word came that the attack upon the hills was to be postponed till after 5p.m. Seeing the danger of delay, and that Chocolate Hill at least should be seized at once, the Brigadier-General (Hill) telephoned for supports and covering fire, held off the attack on his left with one battalion, and with the rest of his brigade started at once to take Chocolate Hill, cost what it might. The men went forward and stormed Chocolate Hill, the 7th Royal Dublin Fusiliers bearing the brunt of the storm.

At some not specified time, perhaps after this storm, in a general retirement of the Turks, Hill 70, or Scimitar Hill, was abandoned to us, and occupied by an English battalion.

During all this day of the 7th of August all our men suffered acutely from the great heat and from thirst. Several men went raving mad from thirst, others assaulted the water guards, pierced the supply hoses, or swam to the lighters to beg for water. Thirst in great heat is a cruel pain, and this (afflicting some regiments more than others) demoralized some and exhausted all. Efforts were made to send up and to find water; but the distribution system, beginning on a cluttered beach and ending in a rough, unknown country full of confused fighting and firing, without anything like a road, and much of it blazing or smouldering from the scrub fires, broke down, and most of the local wells, when discovered, were filled with corpses put there by the Turk garrison. Some unpolluted wells of drinkable, though brackish, water were found; but most of these were guarded by snipers, who shot at men going to them. Many men were killed thus and many more wounded, for the Turk snipers were good shots, cleverly hidden.

All through the day in the Suvla area thirst, due to the great heat, was another cause of loss of time in the fulfilment of that part of the tactical scheme; but it was not the final and fatal cause.

Chocolate Hill was taken by our men (now utterly exhausted by thirst and heat) just as darkness fell. They were unable to go on against Ismail Oglu Tepe. They made their dispositions for the night on the line they had won, sent back to the beaches for ammunition, food, and water, and tried to forget their thirst. They were in bad case, and still two miles from the Australians below Koja Chemen Tepe. Very late that night word reached them that the Turks were massed in a gully to their front, that no other enemy reserves were anywhere visible, and that the Turks had withdrawn their guns, fearing that they would be taken next morning. Before dawn on the all-important day of the 8th of August, our men at Suvla, after a night of thirst and sniping, stood to arms to help out the vital thrust of the battle.

Had time not been lost on the 7th, their task on the 8th would have been to cross the valley at dawn, join the Australians, and go with them up the spurs to victory, in a strength which the Turks could not oppose. At dawn on the 8th their path to the valley was still barred by the uncaptured Turk fort on Ismail; time had been lost; there could be no crossing the valley till Ismail was taken. There was still time to take it and cross the valley to the storm, but the sands were falling. Up on Chunuk already the battle had begun without them; no time was lost on Chunuk.

Up on Chunuk at that moment a very bitter battle was being fought. On the right, on Chunuk itself, the Gloucester and New Zealand Regiments were storming the hill; in the centre and on the left the Australians, English, and Indians were trying for Hill Q and the south of Koja Chemen. They had passed the night on the hill-sides under a never-ceasing fire of shells and bullets; now, before dawn, they were making a terrible attempt. Those on Chunuk went up with a rush, pelted from in front and from both flanks by every engine of death. The Gloucesters were on the left and the New Zealanders on the right in this great assault. They deployed past the Farm, and then went on to the storm of a hill which rises some four hundred feet in as many yards. They were on the top by dawn; Chunuk Bair, the last step but one to victory, was ours, and remained ours all day, but at a cost which few successful attacks have ever known. By four o'clock that afternoon the New Zealanders had dwindled to three officers and fifty men, and the Gloucester battalion, having lost every officer and senior non-commissioned officer, was fighting under section leaders and privates. Still, their attack had succeeded; they were conquerors. In the centre the attack on Hill Q was less successful. There the English and Indian regiments, assaulting together, were held; the Turks were too strong. Our men got up to the top of the lower spurs, and there had to lie down and scrape cover, for there was no going farther. On the left of our attack the Australians tried to storm the Abd-el-Rahman Bair from the big gully of Asma Dere. They went up in the dark with Australian dash to a venture pretty desperate even for Gallipoli. The Turks held the high ground on both sides of the Asma gully, and were there in great force with many machine guns. The Australians were enfiladed, held in front and taken in reverse, and (as soon as it was light enough for the Turks to see) they suffered heavily. As one of the Australians has described it: "The 14th and 15th Battalions moved out in single file and deployed to the storm, and an advance was made under heavy rifle and machine-gun fire. After the 15th Battalion had practically withered away, the 14th continued to advance, suffering heavily, and the Turks in great force. As we drove them back, they counter-attacked, several times. The battalion thus got very split up, and it is impossible to say exactly what happened."

132

It is now possible to say exactly that that 14th Battalion fought like heroes in little bands of wounded and weary men, and at last, with great reluctance, on repeated orders, fell back to the Asma Dere from which they had come, beating off enemy attacks all the way down the hill, and then held on against all that the Turk could do.

By noon, this assault, which would have been decisive had the men from Suvla been engaged with the Australians, was at an end. Its right had won Chunuk, and could just hold on to what it had won; its centre was held, and its left driven back. The fire upon all parts of the line was terrific; our men were lying (for the most part) in scratching of cover, for they could not entrench under fire so terrible. Often in that rough-and-tumble country the snipers and bombers of both sides were within a few yards of each other, and in the roar and blast of the great battle were countless little battles, or duels, to the death, which made the ground red and set the heather on fire. Half of the hills of that accursed battlefield, too false of soil to be called crags and too savage with desolation to be called hills, such as feed the sheep and bees of England, were blazing in sweeps of flame, which cast up smoke to heaven, and swept in great swathes across the gullies. Shells from our ships were screaming and bursting among all that devil's playground; it was an anxious time for the Turks. Many a time throughout that day the Turkish officers must have looked down anxiously upon the Suvla plain to see if our men there were masters of Ismail and on the way to Koja Chemen. For the moment, as they saw, we were held; but not more than held. With a push from Suvla to help us, we could not be held. Our men on the hills, expecting that helping push, drew breath for a new assault.

It was now noon. The battle so far was in our favour. We had won ground, some of it an all-important ground, and for once we had the Turks with their backs against the wall and short of men. At Helles they were pressed, at Lone Pine they were threatened at the heart, under Koja Chemen the knife-point was touching the heart, and at Suvla was the new strength to drive the knife-point home and begin the end of the war. And the Turks could not stop that new strength. Their nearest important reserve of men was at Eski Keui, ten miles away by a road which could scarcely be called a goat track, and these reserves had been called on for the fight at Krithia, and still more for the two days of struggle at Lone Pine. All through that day of the 8th of August Fate waited to see what would happen between Suvla and Koja Chemen. She fingered with her dice, uncertain which side to favour; she waited to be courted by the one who wanted her. Eight hours of daylight had gone by, but there was still no moving forward from Suvla, to seize Ismail and pass from it across the valley to the storm. Noon passed into the afternoon, but there was still no movement. Four hours more went by, and now our aeroplanes brought word that the

Turks near Suvla were moving back their guns by ox-teams, and that their foot were on the march, coming along their break-neck road, making perhaps a mile an hour, but marching and drawing steadily nearer to the threatened point. The living act of the battle was due at Ismail; from Ismail the last act, the toppling down of the Turk for ever among the bones of his victims and the ruin of his Ally, would have been prepared and assured. There was a desultory fire around Ismail and the smoke of scrub fires, which blazed and smouldered everywhere as far as the eye could see, but no roar and blaze and outcry of a meant attack. The battle hung fire on the left, the hours were passing, the Turks were coming. It was only five o'clock still; we had still seven hours or more. In the centre we had almost succeeded. We could hang on there and try again, there was still time. The chance which had been plainly ours was still an even chance. It was for the left to seize it for us: the battle waited for the left; the poor dying Gloucesters and Wellingtons hung on to Chunuk for it; the Gurkhas and English in the trampled cornfields near the Farm died where they lay on the chance of it; the Australians on Abdel-Rahman held steady in the hope of it, under a fire that filled the air.

If, as men say, the souls of a race, all the company of a nation's dead, rally to the living of their people in a time of storm, those fields of hell below Koja Chemen, won by the sweat and blood and dying agony of our thousands, must have answered with a ghostly muster of English souls in the afternoon of that 8th of August. There was the storm, there was the crisis, the one picked hour, to which this death and mangling and dying misery and exultation had led. Then was the hour for a casting off of self, and a setting aside of every pain and longing and sweet affection, a giving up of all that makes a man to the something which makes a race, and a going forward to death resolvedly to help out their brothers high up above in the shell bursts and the blazing gorse. Surely all through the 8th of August our unseen dead were on that field, blowing the horn of Roland, the unheard, unheeded horn, the horn of heroes in the dolorous pass, asking for the little that heroes ask, but asking in vain. If ever the great of England cried from beyond death to the living they cried then. *De ço qui calt. Demuret i unt trop.*

All through the morning of that day the Commander-in-Chief, on watch at his central station, had waited with growing anxiety for the advance from the Suvla beaches. Till the afternoon the critical thrust on Chunuk and the great Turk pressure at Lone Pine made it impossible for him to leave his post to intervene; but in the afternoon, seeing that neither wireless nor telephone messages could take the place of personal vision and appeal, he took the risk of cutting himself adrift from the main conflict, hurried to Suvla, landed, and found the great battle of the war, that should have brought peace to all that Eastern world, being lost by minutes before his eyes.

Only one question mattered then: "Was there still time?" Had the Turks made good their march and crowned those hills, or could our men forestall them? It was now doubtful, but the point was vital, not only to the battle, but to half the world in travail. It had to be put to the test. A hundred years ago, perhaps even fifty years ago, all could have been saved. Often in those old days a Commander-in-Chief could pull a battle out of the fire and bring halted or broken troops to victory. Then, by waving a sword, and shouting a personal appeal, the resolute soul could pluck the hearts of his men forward in a rush that nothing could stem. So Wolfe took Quebec; so Desaix won Marengo; so Bonaparte swept the bridge at Lodi, and won at Arcola; so Cæsar overcame the Nervii in the terrible day, and wrecked the Republic at Pharsalia; so Sherman held the landing at Shiloh, and Farragut pitted his iron heart against iron ships at Fort Jackson; so Sir Ian Hamilton himself snatched victory from the hesitation at Elandslaagte. Then the individual's will could take instant effect. But then the individual's front was not a five-mile front of wilderness; the men were under his hand, within sight and sound of him, and not committed by order to another tactical project. There, at Suvla, was no chance for these heroic methods. Suvla was the modern battlefield, where nothing can be done quickly except the firing of a machine gun. On the modern field, especially on such a field as Suvla, where the troops were scattered in the wilderness, it may take several hours for an order to pass from one wing to the other. In this case it was not an order that was to pass, but a counter-order; the order had already gone, for an attack at dawn on the morrow.

All soldiers seem agreed, that even with authority to back it, a counter-order, on a modern battlefield, to urge forward halted troops, takes time to execute. Sir Ian Hamilton's determination to seize those hills could not spare the time; too much time had already gone. He ordered an advance at all costs with whatever troops were not scattered, but only four battalions could be found in any way ready to move. It was now 5p.m.: there were perhaps three more hours of light. The four battalions were ordered to advance at once to make good what they could of the hills fronting the bay before the Turks forestalled them. At dawn the general attack, as already planned, was to support them. Unfortunately, the four battalions were less ready than was thought; they were not able to advance at once, nor for ten all-precious hours. They did not begin to advance till four o'clock the next morning (the 9th of August), and even then the rest of the division which was to support them was not in concert with them. They attacked the hills to the north of Anafarta Sagir, but they were now too late; the Turks were there before them, in great force, with their guns, and the thrust, which the day before could have been met by (at most) five Turk battalions without artillery, was now parried and thwarted. Presently the division attacked, with great gallantry, over burning scrub, seized Ismail, and was then checked and forced back to the Chocolate Hills. The left had failed. The main blow of the battle on Sari Bair was to have no support from Suvla.

The main blow was given, none the less, by the troops near Chunuk. Three columns were formed in the pitchy blackness of the very early morning of the 9th, two to seize and clear Chunuk and Hill Q, the third to pass from Hill Q on the wave of the assault to the peak of Koja Chemen. The first two columns were on the lower slopes of Chunuk and in the fields about the Farm, with orders to attack at dawn. The third column, consisting wholly of English troops, was not yet on the ground, but moving during the night up the Chailak Dere. The Dere was jammed with pack-mules, ammunition, and wounded men; it was pitch dark, and the column made bad going, and those leading it were doubtful of the way. Brigadier-General Baldwin, who commanded, left his brigade in the Dere, went to the headquarters of the first column, and brought back guides to lead his brigade into position. The guides led him on in the darkness, till they realized that they were lost. The Brigadier marched his men back to the Chailak, and then, still in pitch darkness, up a nullah into the Aghyl Dere, and from there, in growing light, towards the Farm. This wandering in the darkness had tragical results.

At half-past four the guns from the ships and the army opened on Chunuk, and the columns moved to the assault. Soon the peaks of their objective were burning like the hills of hell to light them on their climb to death, and they went up in the half-darkness to the storm of a volcano spouting fire, driving the Turks before them. Some of the Warwicks and South Lancashires were the first upon the top of Chunuk; Major Allanson, leading the 6th Gurkhas, was the first on the ridge between Chunuk and Hill Q. Up on to the crests came the crowding sections; the Turks were breaking and falling back. Our men passed over the crests, and drove the Turks down on the other side. Victory was flooding up over Chunuk like the Severn tide; our men had scaled the scarp, and there below them lay the ditch, the long grey streak of the Hellespont, the victory and the reward of victory. The battle lay like a field ripe to the harvest: our men had but to put in the sickle. The third column was the sickle of that field, that third column which had lost its way in the blackness of the wilderness. Even now that third column was coming up the hill below; in a few minutes it would have been over the crest, going on to victory with the others. Then, at that moment of time, while our handful on the hill-top waited for the weight of the third column to make its thrust a death-blow, came the most tragical thing in all that tragical campaign.

It was barely daylight when our men won the hill-top. The story is that our men moving on the crest were mistaken for Turks, or (as some think) that there was some difference in the officers' watches — some few minutes' delay in beginning the fire of the guns, and therefore some few minutes' delay in stopping the bombardment, which had been ordered to continue upon the crest for three-quarters of an hour from 4.30a.m. Whatever the cause, whether accident, fate, mistake, or the daily waste and confusion of battle, our own guns searched the hill-top for some minutes too long, and thinned out our brave handful with a terrible fire. They were caught in the open and destroyed there; the Turks charged back upon the remnant, and beat them off the greater part of the crest. Only a few minutes after this the third column came into action in support: too late.

The Turks beat them down the hill to the Farm, but could not drive the men of the first column from the south-western half of the top of the Chunuk. All through the hard and bloody day of the 9th of August the Turks tried to carry this peak, but never quite could, though the day was one long succession of Turk attacks, the Turks fresh and in great strength, our men weary from three terrible days and nights and only a battalion strong, since the peak would not hold more. The New Zealanders and some of the 13th Division held that end of Chunuk. They were in trenches which had been dug under fire, partly by themselves, partly by the Turks. In most places these trenches were only scratchings in the ground, since neither side on that blazing and stricken hill could stand to dig. Here and there, in sheltered patches, the trenches were three feet deep, but whether three feet deep or three inches, all were badly sited, and in some parts had only ten yards' field of fire. In these pans or scratchings our men fought all day, often hand to hand, usually under a pelt of every kind of fire, often amid a shower of bombs, since the Turks could creep up under cover to within so few yards. Our men lost very heavily during the day, but at nightfall we still held the peak. After dark the 6th Loyal North Lancashires relieved the garrison, took over the trenches, did what they could to strengthen them, and advanced them by some yards here and there. At four o'clock on the morning of the 10th, the 5th Wiltshires came up to support them, and lay down behind the trenches in the ashes, sand, and scattered rubble of the hill-top. Both battalions were exhausted from four days and nights of continual fighting, but in very good heart. At this time these two battalions marked the extreme right of our new line; on their left, stretching down to the Farm, were the 10th Hampshires, and near the Farm the remains of the third column under General Baldwin. There may have been in all some 5,000 men on Chunuk and within a quarter of a mile of it round the Farm.

In the darkness before dawn, when our men on the hill were busy digging themselves better cover for the day's battle, the Turks, now strongly reinforced from Bulair and Asia, assaulted Chunuk with not less than 15,000 men. They came on in a monstrous mass, packed shoulder to shoulder, in some places eight deep, in others three or four deep. Practically all their first line were shot by our men, practically all the second line were bayoneted, but the third line got into our trenches and overwhelmed the garrison. Our men fell back to the second line of trenches, and rallied and fired; but the Turks overwhelmed that line too, and then with their packed multitude they paused and gathered like a wave, burst down on the Wiltshire Regiment, and destroyed it almost to a man. Even so, the survivors, outnumbered forty to one, formed and charged with the bayonet, and formed and charged a second time, with a courage which makes the charge of the Light Brigade seem like a dream. But it was a hopeless position. The Turks came on like the sea, beat back all before them, paused for a moment, set rolling down the hill upon our men a number of enormous round bombs, which bounded into our lines and burst, and then following up this artillery they fell on the men round the Farm in the most bloody and desperate fight of the campaign.

Even as they topped Chunuk and swarmed down to engulf our right, our guns opened upon them in a fire truly awful; but thousands came alive over the crest, and went down to the battle below. Stragglers running from the first rush put a panic in the Aghyl Dere, where bearers, doctors, mules, and a multitude of wounded were jammed up with soldiers trying to get up to the fight. Some of our men held up against this thrust of the Turks, and in that first brave stand General Baldwin was killed. Then our line broke, the Turks got fairly in among our men with a weight which bore all before it, and what followed was a long succession of British rallies to a tussle body to body, with knives and stones and teeth — a fight of wild beasts in the ruined cornfields of the Farm. Nothing can be said of that fight, no words can describe nor any mind imagine it, except as a roaring and blazing hour of killing. Our last reserves came up to it, and the Turks were beaten back; very few of their men reached their lines alive. The Turk dead lay in thousands all down the slopes of the hill; but the crest of the hill, the prize, remained in Turk hands, not in ours.

That ended the battle of the 6th to 10th of August. We had beaten off the Turks, but our men were too much exhausted to do more. They could not go up the hill again. Our thrust at Sari Bair had failed. It had just failed, by a few minutes, though unsupported from the left. Even then, at the eleventh hour, two fresh battalions and a ton of water would have made Chunuk ours; but we had neither the men nor the water. Sari was not to be our hill. Our men fought for four days and nights in a wilderness of gorse and precipice to make her ours. They fought in a blazing sun, without rest, with little food and with almost no water, on hills on fire and on crags rotting to the tread. They went, like all their brothers in that Peninsula, on a forlorn hope, and by bloody pain they won the image and the taste of victory; and then, when their reeling bodies had burst the bars, so that our race might pass through, there were none to pass; the door was open, but there were none to go through it to triumph. And then, slowly, as strength failed, the door was shut again, the bars were forged again, victory was hidden again, all was to do again, and our brave men were but the fewer and the bitterer for all their bloody sacrifice for the land they served. All was to do again after the 10th of August; the great battle of the campaign was over. We had made our fight, we had seen our enemy beaten and the prize displayed, and then (as before at Helles) we had to stop for want of men, till the enemy had remade his army and rebuilt his fort.

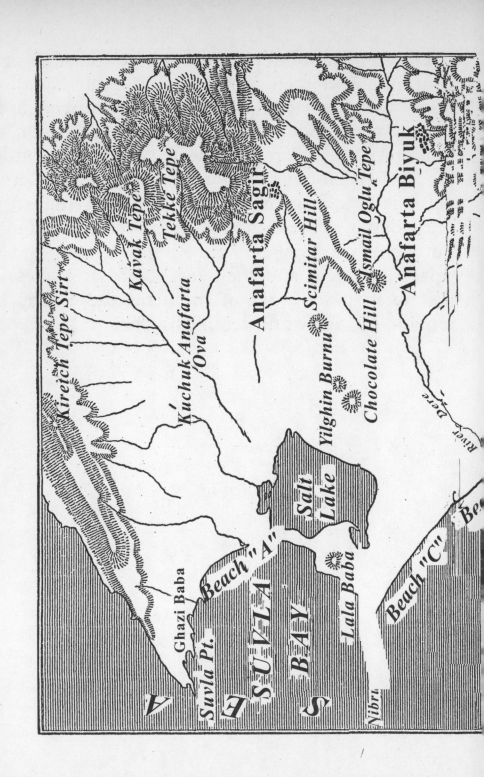

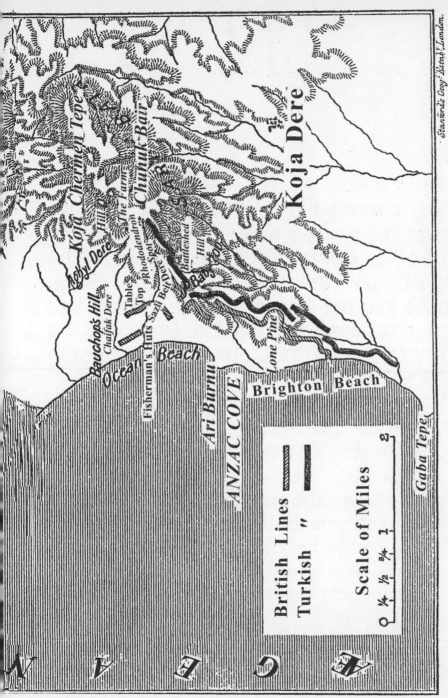

Stanfords Geog¹ Estab.ᵗ London.

ANZAC-SUVLA.

Koja Chemen Tepe

Koja Dere

Chunuk Bair

Hill

The Farm

Abdyl Dere

"Rhododendron Spot"

Table Top

Battleshed Hill

Sazli Beit Dere

Baby 700

Bauchops Hill

Chaifak Dere

Fisherman's Huts

Ocean Beach

Lone Pine

Ari Burnu

ANZAC COVE

Brighton Beach

Gaba Tepe

N   E   G   E   A   N

British Lines
Turkish "

Scale of Miles

0   ¼   ½   ¾   1   2

CHAPTER
SIX

The day passed, the night came, the King lay down in his vaulted room. St. Gabriel came from God to call him. "Charles, summon the army of your Empire, and go by forced marches into the land of Bire, to the city that the pagans have besieged. The Christians call and cry for you." The Emperor wished not to go. "God," he said. "How painful is my life!" He wept from his eyes, he tore his white beard.
— *The End of the Song of Roland*.

That, in a way, was the end of the campaign, for no other attempt to win through was made. The Turks were shaken to the heart. Another battle following at once might well have broken them. But we had not the men nor the shells for another battle. In the five days' battle on the front of twelve miles we had lost very little less than a quarter of our entire army, and we had shot away most of our always scanty supply of ammunition. We could not attack again till 50,000 more men were landed and the store of shells replenished. Those men and shells were not

148

near Gallipoli, but in England, where the war as a whole had to be considered. The question to be decided, by those directing the war as a whole, was, "Should those men and shells be sent?" It was decided by the High Direction that they should not be sent; the effort, therefore, could not be made.

Since the effort could not be made, the campaign declined into a secondary operation — to contain large reserves of Turks, with their guns and munitions, from use elsewhere, in Mesopotamia or in the Caucasus. But before it became this, a well-planned and well-fought effort was made from Suvla to secure our position by seizing the hills to the east of the Bay. This attack took place on the 21st of August, in intense heat, across an open plain without cover of any kind, blazing throughout nearly all its length with scrub fires. The 29th Division (brought up from Cape Helles) carried Scimitar Hill with great dash, and was then held up. The attack on Ismail Oglu failed. Two thrusts, made by the men of Anzac in the latter days of August, secured an important well and the Turk stronghold of Hill 60. This last success made the line from Anzac to Suvla impregnable.

After this, since no big attempt could be made by the Allied troops, and no big attempt was made by the enemy, the fighting settled down into trench warfare on both sides. There was some shelling every day and night, some machine-gun and rifle fire, much sniping, great vigilance, and occasional bombing and mining. The dysentery, which had been present ever since the heats began, increased beyond all measure: very few men in all that army were not attacked and weakened by it. Many thousands went down with it; Mudros, Alexandria, and Malta were filled with cases; many died.

Those who remained, besides carrying on the war by daily and nightly fire, worked continually with pick and shovel to improve the lines. Long after the war, the goatherd on Gallipoli will lose his way in the miles of trenches which zigzag from Cape Helles to Achi Baba and from Gaba Tepe to Ejelmer Bay. They run to and fro in all that expanse of land, some of them shallow, others deep cuttings in the marl, many of them paved with stone or faced with concrete, most of them sided with little caverns, leading far down (in a few cases) to rooms twenty feet under the ground. Long after we are all dust, the goats of Gallipoli will break their legs in those pits and ditches, and over their coffee round the fire the elders will say that they were dug by devils and the sons of devils, and antiquarians will come from the West to dig there, and will bring away shards of iron and empty tins and bones. Fifty years ago some French staff officers traced out the works round Durazzo, where Pompey the Great fought just such another campaign, two thousand years ago. Two thousand years hence, when this war is forgotten, those lines under the ground will draw the staff officers of whatever country is then the most cried for brains.

Those lines were the homes of thousands of our soldiers for half a year and more. There they lived and did their cooking and washing, made their jokes and sang their songs. There they sweated under their burdens, and slept, and fell in to die. There they marched up the burning hill, where the sand devils flung by the shells were blackening heaven; there they lay in their dirty rags awaiting death; and there by thousands up and down they lie buried, in little lonely graves where they fell, or in the pits of the great engagements.

Those lines at Cape Helles, Anzac, and Suvla, were once busy towns, thronged by thousands of citizens, whose going and coming and daily labour were cheerful with singing, as though those places were mining camps during a gold rush, instead of a perilous front where the fire never ceased and the risk of death was constant. But for the noise of war, coming in an irregular rattle, with solitary big explosions, the screams of shells, or the wild whistling crying of ricochets, they seemed busy but very peaceful places. At night, from the sea, the lamps of the dugouts on the cliffs were like the lights of sea-coast towns in summer, and the places seemingly as peaceful, but for the pop and rattle of fire and the streaks of glare from the shells. There was always singing, sometimes very good and always beautiful, coming in the crash of war; and always one heard the noises of the work of men — the beat of pile-drivers, wheels going over stones, and the

151

little solid pobbing noises, from bullets dropping in the sea.

I have said that those positions were like mining camps during a gold rush. Ballarat, the Sacramento, and the camps of the Transvaal, must have looked strangely like those camps at Suvla and Cape Helles. Anzac at night was like those crags of old building over the Arno at Florence; by day it was a city of cliff dwellers, stirring memories of the race's past. An immense expanse was visible from all these places: at Cape Helles there was the plain rising gradually to Achi Baba, at Anzac a wilderness of hills, at Suvla the same hills seen from below. Over all these places came a strangeness of light, unlike anything to be seen in the West, a light which made the hills clear and unreal at the same time, softening their savagery into peace, till they seemed not hills but swellings of the land, as though the land there had breathed in and risen a little. All the places were dust-coloured as soon as the flowers had withered, a dark dust-colour where the scrub grew (often almost wine-dark like our own hills where heather grows), a pale sand colour where the scrub gave out, and elsewhere a paleness and a greyness as of moss and lichen and old stone. On this sandy and dusty land, where even the trees were grey and ghostly (olive and Eastern currant), the camps were scattered, a little and a little, never much in one place on account of shelling, till the impression given was one of multitude.

The signs of the occupation began far out at sea, where the hospital ships lay waiting for their freight. There were always some there, painted white and green, lying outside the range of the big guns. Nearer to the shore were the wrecks of ships, some of them sunk by our men, to make breakwaters, some sunk by the Turk shells, some knocked to pieces or washed ashore by foul weather. Nearly all these wrecks were of small size, trawlers, drifters, and little coastwise vessels such as peddle and bring home fish on the English coasts. Closer in, right on the beaches, were the bones of still smaller boats, pinnaces, cutters, and lighters, whose crews had been the men of the first landings. Men could not see those wrecks without a thrill. There were piers at all the beaches, all built under shell fire, to stand both shell fire and the sea, and at the piers there was always much busy life, men singing at their work, horses and mules disembarking, food and munitions and water discharging, wounded going home and drafts coming ashore. On the beaches were the hieroglyphs of the whole bloody and splendid story; there were the marks and signs, which no one could mistake nor see unmoved.

Even after months of our occupation the traces were there off the main tracks. A man had but to step from one of the roads into the scrub, and there they lay, relics of barbed wire (blown aside in tangles), round shrapnel-bullets in the sand, empty cartridge-cases, clips of cartridge-cases bent double by a blow yet undischarged, pieces of flattened rifle barrel, rags of leather, broken bayonets, jags and hacks of shell, and, in little hollows, little heaps of cartridge-cases where some man had lain to fire for hour after hour, often until he died at his post, on the 25th of April. Here, too, one came upon the graves of soldiers, sometimes alone, sometimes three or four together, each with an inscribed cross and border of stones from the beach. Privates, sergeants, and officers lay in those graves, and by them, all day long, the work, which they had made possible by that sacrifice on the 25th, went on in a stream, men and munitions going up to the front, and wounded and the dying coming down, while the explosions of the cannon trembled through the earth to them, and the bullets piped and fell over their heads.

But the cities of those camps were not cities of the dead, they were cities of intense life, cities of comradeship and resolve, unlike the cities of peace. At Mudros, all things seemed little, for there men were dwarfed by their setting; they were there in ships, which made even a full battalion seem only a cluster of heads. On the Peninsula they seemed to have come for the first time to full stature. There they were bigger than their surroundings. There they were naked manhood pitted against death in the desert, and more than holding their own.

All those sun-smitten hills and gullies, growing nothing but crackling scrub, were peopled by crowds. On all the roads, on the plain, which lay white like salt in the glare, and on the sides of the gullies, strange, sunburned, half-naked men moved at their work with the bronze bodies of gods. Like Egyptians building a city, they passed and repassed with boxes from the walls of stores built on the beach. Dust had toned their uniforms even with the land. Their half-nakedness made them more grand than clad men. Very few of them were less than beautiful; whole battalions were magnificent, the very flower of the world's men. They had a look in their eyes which those who saw them will never forget.

Sometimes, as one watched, one heard a noise of cheering from the ships, and this, the herald of good news, passed inland, till men would rise from sleep in their dug-outs, come to the door, blinking in the sun, to pass on the cheer. In some strange way the news, the cause of the cheering, passed inland with the cheer, a submarine had sunk a transport off Constantinople, or an aeroplane had bombed a powder factory. One heard the news pass on and on, till it rang from the front trenches ten yards from the Turk line. Sometimes the cheering was very loud, mingled with singing; then it was a new battalion, coming from England, giving thanks that they were there, after their months of training, to help the fleet through. Men who heard those battalions singing will never hear those songs of "Tipperary," "Let's all go down the Strand," or

"We'll all go the same way home," without a quickening at the heart.

Everywhere in the three positions there were the homes of men. In gashes or clefts of the earth were long lines of mules or horses with Indian grooms. On the beaches were offices, with typewriters clicking and telephone bells ringing. Stacked on one side were ammunition-carts so covered with bushes that they looked like the scrub they stood on. Here and there were strangely painted guns, and everywhere the work of men, armourer's forges, farrier's anvils, the noise and clink and bustle of a multitude. Everywhere, too, but especially in the gullies, were the cave-dwellings of the dug-outs, which so dotted the cliffs with their doors that one seemed put back to Cro-Magnon or Tampa, into some swarming tribe of cave-dwellers. All the dug-outs were different, though all were built upon the same principle, first a scooping in the earth, then a raised earth ledge for a bed, then (if one were lucky) a corrugated iron roof propped by balks, lastly a topping of sandbags strewn with scrub. For doors, if one had a door or sunshade, men used sacking, burlap, a bit of canvas, or a blanket. Then, when the work was finished, the builder entered in, to bathe in his quarter of a pint of water, smoke his pipe, greet his comrades, and think foul scorn of the Turk, whose bullets piped and droned overhead, all day and night, like the little finches of home. Looking out from the upper dug-outs, one saw the dusty, swarming warren of men, going and coming, with a kind of swift slouch, carrying boxes from the beach. Mules and men passed; songs went up and down the gullies, and were taken up by those at rest; men washed and mended clothes, or wandered naked and sun-reddened along the beach, bathing among dropping bullets. Wounded men came down on stretchers, sick men babbled in pain or cursed the flies, the forges clinked, the pile-drivers beat in the balks of the piers, the bullets droned and piped, or rushed savagely, or pobbed into a sandbag. Up in the trenches the rifles made the irregular snaps of fire-crackers, sometimes almost ceasing, then popping, then running along a section in a rattle, then quickening down the line and drawing the enemy, then pausing and slowly ceasing and beginning again. From time to time, with a whistle and a wailing, some Asian shell came over, and drooped and seemed to multiply, and gathered to herself the shriek of all the devils of hell, and burst like a devil, and filled a great space with blackness and dust and falling fragments. Then another and another came, almost in the same place, till the gunners had had enough. Then the dust settled, the ruin was made good, and all went on as before, men carrying and toiling and singing, bullets piping, and the flies settling and swarming on whatever was obscene in what the shell had scattered.

Everywhere in those positions there was gaiety and courage and devoted brotherhood; but there was also another thing, which brooded over all, and struck right home to the heart. It was a tragical feeling, a taint or flavour in the mind, such as men often feel in hospitals when many are dying, the sense that Death was at work there, that Death lived there, that Death wandered up and down there and fed on Life.

Since the main object of the campaign, to help the fleet through the Narrows, had been abandoned (in mid-August), and no further thrust was to be made against the Turks, the questions, "Were our 100,000 men in Gallipoli containing a sufficiently large army of Turks to justify their continuance on the Peninsula?" and "Could they be more profitably used elsewhere?" arose in the minds of the High Direction from week to week as the war changed and increased.

In the early autumn, when the Central Powers combined with Bulgaria to crush Serbia and open a road to Constantinople, these questions became acute. During October, owing to the radical change in the Balkan situation, which was produced by the treachery of Bulgaria and the bewildering indecision of Greece, the advantage of our continuing the campaign became more and more doubtful; and in November, after full consideration, it was decided to evacuate the Peninsula. Preparations were made and the work begun.

Late in November something happened which had perhaps some influence in hurrying on the date of the evacuation. This was the blizzard of the 26th to 28th, which lost us about a tenth of our whole army from cold, frost-bite, exposure, and the sicknesses which follow them. The 26th began as a cold, dour Gallipoli day with a bitter north-easterly wind, which increased in the afternoon to a fresh gale, with sleet. Later, it increased still more, and blew hard, with thunder; and with the thunder came a rain more violent than any man of our army had ever seen. Water pours off very quickly from that land of abrupt slopes. In a few minutes every gully was a raging torrent, and every trench a river. By an ill-chance this storm fell with cruel violence upon the ever famous 29th Division, then holding trenches at Suvla. The water poured down into their trenches as though it were a tidal wave. It came in with a rush, with a head upon it like the tide advancing, so quickly that men were one minute dry and the next moment drowned at their posts. They were caught so suddenly that those who escaped had to leap from their trenches for dear life, leaving coats, haversacks, food, and sometimes even their rifles, behind them.

Our trenches were in nearly every case below those of the Turks, who therefore suffered from the water far less than our men did. The Turks saw our men leaping from their trenches, and, either guessing the reason or fearing an attack, opened a very heavy rifle and shrapnel fire upon them. Our men had to shelter behind the parados of their trenches, where they scraped themselves shallow pans in the mud under a heavy fire. At dark the sleet increased, the mud froze, and there our men lay, most of them without overcoats, and many of them without food. In one trench when the flood rose, a pony, a mule, a pig, and two dead Turks were washed over a barricade together.

Before the night fell, many of our men were frost-bitten, and started limping to the ambulances, under continual shrapnel fire and in blinding sleet. A good many fell down by the way, and were frozen to death. The gale increased slowly all through the night, blowing hard and steadily from the north, making a great sea upon the coast, and driving the spray far inland. At dawn it grew colder, and the sleet hardened into snow, with an ever-increasing wind, which struck through our men to the marrow. "They fell ill," said one who was there, "in heaps." The water from the flood had fallen in the night, but it was still four feet deep in many of the trenches, and our men passed the morning under fire in their shelter pans, fishing for food and rifles in their drowned lines. All through the day the wind gathered, till it was blowing a full gale, vicious and bitter cold; and on the 28th it reached its worst. The 28th was spoken of afterwards as "Frozen Foot Day"; it was a day more terrible than any battle. But now it was taking toll of the Turks, and the fire slackened. Probably either side could have had the other's position for the taking on the 28th, had there been enough unfrosted feet to advance. It was a day so blind with snow and driving storm that neither side could see to fire, and this brought the advantage, that our men, hopping to the ambulances, had not to go through a pelt of shrapnel bullets. On the 29th, the limits of human strength were reached. Some of those frozen three days before were able to return to duty, but "a great number of officers and men who had done their best to stick it out were forced to go to hospital." The water fell during this day, but it left on an average two and a half feet of thick, slushy mud, into which many trenches collapsed. After this the weather was fine and warm.

At Helles and Anzac the fall of the ground gave some protection from this gale, but at Suvla there was none. When the weather cleared, the beaches were heaped with the wreck of piers, piles, boats and lighters, all broken and jammed together. But great as this wreck was, the wreck of men was even greater. The 29th Division had lost two-thirds of its strength. In the three sectors over 200 men were dead, over 10,000 were unfit for further service, and not less than 30,000 others were sickened and made old by it.

The Turk loss was much more serious even than this, for though they suffered less from the wet, they suffered more from the cold, through being on the higher ground. The snow lay upon their trenches long after it had gone from ours, and the Turk equipment, though very good as far as it went, was only good for the summer. Their men wore thin clothes, and many of them had neither overcoat nor blanket. The blizzard, which was a discouragement to us, took nearly all the heart out of the Turks; and this fact must be borne in mind in the reading of the next few pages.

The gale had one good effect: either the cold or the rain destroyed or removed the cause of the dysentery, which had taken nearly a thousand victims a day for some months. The disease stopped at once, and no more fresh cases were reported.

This storm made any attempt to land or to leave the land impossible for four days together. Coming, as it did, upon the decision to evacuate, it gave the prompting, that the evacuation should be hurried, lest such weather should prevent it. On the 8th of December, the evacuation of Anzac and Suvla was ordered to begin.

It was not an easy task to remove large numbers of men, guns, and animals from positions commanded by the Turk observers, and open to every cruising aeroplane. But by ruse and skill, and the use of the dark, favoured by fine weather, the work was done, almost without loss, and, as far as one could judge, unsuspected.

German agents, eager to discredit those whom they could not defeat, have said "that we bribed the Turks to let us go"; next year, perhaps, they will say "that the Turks bribed us to go"; the year after that, perhaps, they will invent something equally false and even sillier. But putting aside the foulness and the folly of this bribery lie, it is interesting to inquire how it happened that the Turks did not attack our men while they were embarking.

The Turks were very good fighters, furious in attack and resolute in defence, but among their qualities of mind were some which greatly puzzled our commanders. Their minds would sometimes work in ways very strange to Europeans. They did, or refrained from doing, certain things in ways for which neither we nor our Allies could account. Some day, long hence, when the war is over, the Turk story of our withdrawal will be made known. Until then, we can only guess why it was that the embarkation, which many had thought would lose us half our army, was made good from Anzac and Suvla with the loss of only four or five men (or less than the normal loss of a night in the trenches). Only two explanations are possible. Either (1) the Turks knew that we were going, and wanted to be rid of us; or (2) they did not know that we were going, and were entirely deceived by our ruses.

Had they known that we were going from Anzac and Suvla, it is at least likely that they would have hastened our going, partly that they might win some booty, which they much needed, or take a large number of prisoners, whose appearance would have greatly cheered the citizens of Constantinople. But nearly all those of our army who were there felt, both from observation and intelligence, that the Turks did not know that we were going. As far as men on one side in a war can judge of their enemies, they felt that the Turks were deceived, completely deceived, by the ruses employed by us, and that they believed that we were being strongly reinforced for a new attack. Our soldiers took great pains to make them believe this. Looking down upon us from their heights, the Turks saw boats leaving the shore apparently empty, and returning, apparently, full of soldiers. Looking up at them, from our position our men saw how the sight affected them. For the twelve days during which the evacuation was in progress at Anzac and Suvla, the Turks were plainly to be seen, digging everywhere to secure themselves from the feared attack. They dug new lines, they brought up new guns, they made ready for us in every way. On the night of the 19th-20th December, in hazy weather, at full moon, our men left Suvla and Anzac unmolested.

It was said by Dr. Johnson that "no man does anything, consciously for the last time, without a feeling of sadness." No man of all that force passed down those trenches, the scenes of so much misery and pain and joy and valour and devoted brotherhood, without a deep feeling of sadness. Even those who had been loudest in their joy at going were sad. Many there did not want to go, but felt that it was better to stay, and that then, with another 50,000 men, the task could be done, and their bodies and their blood buy victory for us. This was the feeling even at Suvla, where the men were shaken and sick still from the storm; but at Anzac, the friendly little kindly city, which had been won at such cost in the ever-glorious charge of the 25th, and held since with such pain, and built with such sweat and toil and anguish, in thirst, and weakness, and bodily suffering, which had seen the thousands of the 13th Division land in the dark and hide, and had seen them fall in with the others to go to Chunuk, and had known all the hope and fervour, all the glorious resolve, and all the bitterness and disappointment of the unhelped attempt, the feeling was far deeper. Officers and men went up and down the well-known gullies moved almost to tears by the thought that the next day those narrow acres so hardly won and all those graves of our people so long defended would be in Turk hands.

For some weeks our men had accustomed the Turks to sudden cessations of fire for half an hour or more. At first the Turks had been made suspicious by these silences, but they were now used to them, and perhaps glad of them. They were not made suspicious by the slackening of the fire on the night of the withdrawal. The mules and guns had all gone from Suvla. A few mules and a few destroyed guns were left at Anzac; in both places a pile of stores was left, all soaked in oil and ready for firing. The ships of war drew near to the coast, and trained their guns on the hills. In the haze of the full moon the men filed off from the trenches down to the beaches, and passed away from Gallipoli, from the unhelped attempt which they had given their bodies and their blood to make. They had lost no honour. They were not to blame, that they were creeping off in the dark, like thieves in the night. Had others (not of their profession), many hundreds of miles away, but been as they, as generous, as wise, as foreseeing, as full of sacrifice, those thinned companies with the looks of pain in their faces, and the mud of the hills thick upon their bodies, would have given thanks in Santa Sophia three months before. They had failed to take Gallipoli, and the mine-fields still barred the Hellespont, but they had fought a battle such as has never been seen upon this earth. What they had done will become a glory for ever, wherever the deeds of heroic unhelped men are honoured and pitied and understood. They went up at the call of duty, with a bright banner of a battle-cry, against an impregnable fort. Without guns, without munitions, without help, and without drink, they climbed the scarp, and held it by their own glorious manhood, quickened by a word from their chief. Now they were giving back the scarp, and going out into new adventures, wherever the war might turn.

Those going down to the beaches wondered in a kind of awe whether the Turks would discover them and attack. The minutes passed, and boat after boat left the shore, but no attack came. The arranged rifles fired mechanically in the outer trenches at long intervals, and the crackle of the Turk reply followed. At Anzac, a rearguard of honour had been formed. The last two hundred men to leave Anzac were survivors of those who had landed in the first charge, so glorious and so full of hope, on the 25th of April. They had fought through the whole campaign from the very beginning; they had seen it all. It was only just that they should be the last to leave. As they, too, moved down, one of their number saw a solitary Turk, black against the sky, hard at work upon his trench. That was the last enemy to be seen from Anzac.

At half-past five in the winter morning of the 20th of December the last boat pushed off, and the last of our men had gone from Suvla and Anzac. Those who had been there from the first were deeply touched. There was a longing that it might be to do again, with the same comrades, under the same chiefs, but with better luck and better backing. Some distance from the shore the boats paused to watch the last act in the withdrawal. It was dead calm weather, with just that ruffle of wind which comes before the morning. The Turk fire crackled along the lines as usual, but the withdrawal was still not suspected. Then from the beaches within the stacks of abandoned stores came the noise of explosion; the charges had been fired, and soon immense flames were licking up those boxes and reddening the hills. As the flames grew, there came a stir in the Turk lines, and then every Turk gun that could be brought to bear opened with shrapnel and high explosive on the area of the bonfires. It was plain that the Turks misread the signs. They thought that some lucky shell had fired our stores, and that they could stop us from putting out the flames. Helped by the blasts of many shells, the burning rose like bale-fire, crowned by wreaths and streaks and spouts of flame. The stores were either ashes or in a blaze which none could quench before the Turks guessed the meaning of that burning. Long before the fires had died and before the Turks were wandering in joy among our trenches, our men were aboard their ships standing over to Mudros.

Some have said: "Even if the Turks were deceived at Anzac and Suvla, they must have known that you were leaving Cape Helles. Why did they not attack you while you were embarking there?" I do not know the answer to this question. But it is possible that they did not know that we were leaving. It is possible that they believed that we should hold Cape Helles like an Eastern Gibraltar. It is possible, on the other hand, that they were deceived again by our ruses. It is, however, certain that they watched us far more narrowly at Cape Helles after the Anzac evacuation. Aeroplanes cruised over our position frequently, and shell fire increased and became very heavy. Still, when the time came, the burning of our stores, after our men had embarked, seemed to be the first warning that the Turks had that we were going.

This was a mystery to our soldiers at the time, and seems strange now. It is possible that at Cape Helles the Turks' shaken, frozen, and out-of-heart soldiers may have known that we were going, yet had no life left in them for an attack. Many things are possible in this world, and the darkness is strange, and the heart of a fellow-man is darkness to us. There were things in the Turk heart very dark indeed to those who tried to read it. The storm had dealt with them cruelly, that is all that we know. Let us wait till we know their story.

The Cape Helles position was held for twenty days after we had left Anzac and Suvla. On the 8th-9th of January in the present year, it was abandoned, with slight loss, though in breaking weather. By four o'clock on the morning of the 9th of January, the last man had passed the graves of those who had won the beaches. They climbed on board their boats and pushed off. They had said good-bye to the English dead, whose blood had given them those acres, now being given back. Some felt, as they passed those graves, that the stones were living men, who cast a long look after them when they had passed, and sighed, and turned landward, as they had turned of old. Then in a rising sea, whipped with spray, among the noise of ships weltering to the rails, the battalions left Cape Helles; the *River Clyde* dimmed into the gale and became a memory, and the Gallipoli campaign was over.

Many people have asked me what the campaign achieved. It achieved much. It destroyed and put out of action many more of the enemy than of our own men. Our own losses in killed, wounded, and missing were, roughly speaking, 115,000 and in sick about 100,000 more, or (in all) more than two and one-half times as many as the army which made the landing. The Turk losses from all causes were far greater; they had men to waste, and wasted them, like water, at Cape Helles, Lone Pine, and Chunuk. The real Turk losses will never be tabled and published, but at the five battles of the Landings, the 6th of May, the 4th of June, the 28th of June, and the 6th to 10th of August, they lost in counted killed alone very nearly as many as were killed on our side in the whole campaign. Then, though we did not do what we hoped to do, our presence in Gallipoli contained large armies of Turks in and near the Peninsula. They had always from 15,000 to 20,000 more men than we had on the Peninsula itself, and at least as many more, ready to move, on the Asian shore and at Rodosto. In all, we disabled, or held from action elsewhere, not less than 400,000 Turks, that is, a very large army of men who might have been used elsewhere, with disastrous advantage, in the Caucasus, when Russia was hard pressed, or, as they were used later, in Mesopotamia.

So much for the soldiers' side. But politically, the campaign achieved much. In the beginning, it had a profound effect upon Italy; it was, perhaps, one of the causes which brought Italy into her war with Austria. In the beginning, too, it had a profound effect upon the Balkan States. Bulgaria made no move against us until five months after our landings Had we not gone to Gallipoli, she would have joined our enemies in the late spring instead of in the middle autumn.

Some of our enemies have said that "the campaign was a defeat for the British navy." It is true that we lost two capital ships, from mines, in the early part of the campaign, and I think, in all, two others, from torpedoes, during the campaign. Such loss is not very serious in eleven months of naval war. For the campaign was a naval war; it depended utterly and solely upon the power of the navy. By our navy we went there and were kept there, and by our navy we came away. During the nine months of our hold on the Peninsular, over 300,000 men were brought by the navy from places three, four, or even six thousand miles away. During the operations some half of these were removed by our navy, as sick and wounded, to ports from five hundred to three thousand miles away. Every day for eleven months, ships of our navy moved up and down the Gallipoli coast bombarding the Turk positions. Every day during the operations our navy kept our armies in food, drink, and supplies. Every day, in all that time, if weather permitted, ships of our navy cruised in the Narrows and off Constantinople, and the seaplanes of our navy raided and scouted within the Turk lines. If there had been, I will not say any defeat of, but any check to, the navy, we could not have begun the campaign or continued it. Every moment of those eleven months of war was an illustration of the silent and unceasing victory of our navy's power. As Sir Jan Hamilton has put it, "the navy was our father and mother."

"Still," our enemies say, "you did not win the Peninsular." We did not; and some day, when truth

171

will walk clear-eyed, it will be known why we did not. Until then, let our enemies say this; "They did not win, but they came across three thousand miles of sea, a little army without reserves and short of munitions, a band of brothers, not half of them half-trained, and nearly all of them new to war. They came to what we said was an impregnable fort, on which our veterans of war and massacre had laboured for two sheer months, and by sheer naked manhood they beat us, and drove us out of it. Then rallying, but without reserves, they beat us again, and drove us farther. Then rallying once more, but still without reserves, they beat us again, this time to our knees. Then, had they had reserves, they would have conquered, but by God's pity they had none. Then, after a lapse of time, when we were men again, they had reserves, and they hit us a staggering blow, which needed but a push to end us, but God again had pity. After that our God was indeed pitiful, for England made no further thrust, and they went away.

"Even so was wisdom proven blind,
So courage failed, so strength was chained;
Even so the gods, whose seeing mind
Is not as ours, ordained."

ISIS publish a wide range of books in large print, from fiction to biography. Any suggestions for books you would like to see in large print or audio are always welcome. Please send to the Editorial department at:

ISIS Publishing Ltd.
7 Centremead
Osney Mead
Oxford OX2 0ES
(01865) 250 333

A full list of titles is available free of charge from:
Ulverscroft large print books

(UK)
The Green
Bradgate Road, Anstey
Leicester LE7 7FU
Tel: (0116) 236 4325

(Australia)
P.O Box 953
Crows Nest
NSW 1585
Tel: (02) 9436 2622

(USA)
1881 Ridge Road
P.O Box 1230, West Seneca,
N.Y. 14224-1230
Tel: (716) 674 4270

(Canada)
P.O Box 80038
Burlington
Ontario L7L 6B1
Tel: (905) 637 8734

(New Zealand)
P.O Box 456
Feilding
Tel: (06) 323 6828

Details of **ISIS** complete and unabridged audio books are also available from these offices. Alternatively, contact your local library for details of their collection of **ISIS** large print and unabridged audio books.